4

College
Writing

4

College Writing

HOUGHTON MIFFLIN
ENGLISH FOR ACADEMIC SUCCESS

Li-Lee Tunceren
St. Petersburg College

Sharon L. Cavusgil
Georgia State University

SERIES EDITORS

Patricia Byrd
Joy M. Reid
Cynthia M. Schuemann

Houghton Mifflin Company
Boston   New York

Publisher: Patricia A. Coryell
Director of ESL Publishing: Susan Maguire
Senior Development Editor: Kathy Sands Boehmer
Editorial Assistant: Evangeline Bermas
Senior Project Editor: Kathryn Dinovo
Manufacturing Assistant: Karmen Chong
Senior Marketing Manager: Annamarie Rice
Marketing Assistant: Andrew Whitacre

Cover graphics: LMA Communications, Natick, Massachusetts

Photo credits: © Pete Saloutos/Corbis, top p. 46; © Corbis SYGMA, bottom left p. 46;
© CDC/PHIL/Corbis, bottom center p. 46; © CDC/PHIL/Corbis, bottom right p. 46;
© Royalty-Free/Corbis, p. 94; © Raymond Gehman/Corbis, p. 142

Printed in the U.S.A.

Library of Congress Control Number: 2004112260

ISBN: 0-618-23031-9

23456789-CRW-08 07 06 05

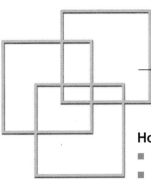

Contents

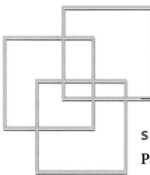

Houghton Mifflin English for Academic Success Series

SERIES EDITORS

Patricia Byrd, Joy M. Reid, Cynthia M. Schuemann

☐ What Is the Purpose of This Series?

The Houghton Mifflin English for Academic Success series is a comprehensive program of student and instructor materials: four levels of student language proficiency textbooks in three skill areas (oral communication, reading, and writing) with supplemental vocabulary textbooks at each level. For instructors and students, a useful website supports classroom teaching, learning, and assessment. For instructors, four Essentials of Teaching Academic Language books (*Essentials of Teaching Academic Oral Communication, Essentials of Teaching Academic Reading, Essentials of Teaching Academic Writing,* and *Essentials of Teaching Academic Vocabulary*) provide helpful information for instructors new to teaching oral communication, reading, writing, and vocabulary.

The fundamental purpose of the series is to prepare students who are not native speakers of English for academic success in U.S. college degree programs. By studying these materials, students in college English for Academic Purposes (EAP) courses will gain the academic language skills they need to be successful students in degree programs. Additionally, students will learn about being successful students in U.S. college courses.

The series is based on considerable prior research as well as our own investigations of students' needs and interests, instructors' needs and desires, and institutional expectations and requirements. For example, our survey research revealed what problems instructors feel they face in their classrooms and what they actually teach; who the students are and what they know and do not know about the "culture" of U.S. colleges; and what types of exams are required for admission at various colleges.

Student Audience

The materials in this series are for college-bound ESL students at U.S. community colleges and undergraduate programs at other institutions. Some of these students are U.S. high school graduates. Some of them are long-term U.S. residents who graduated from a high school before coming to the United States. Others are newer U.S. residents. Still others are more typical international students. All of them need to develop academic language skills and knowledge of ways to be successful in U.S. college degree courses.

All of the books in this series have been created to implement the Houghton Mifflin English for Academic Success competencies. These competencies are based on those developed by ESL instructors and administrators in Florida, California, and Connecticut and are the underlying structure for EAP courses at colleges in those states. These widely respected competencies assure that the materials meet the real world needs of EAP students and instructors.

All of the books focus on . . .

- Starting where the students are, building on their strengths and prior knowledge (which is considerable, if not always academically relevant), and helping students self-identify needs and plans to strengthen academic language skills
- Academic English, including development of academic vocabulary and grammar required by students for academic speaking/listening, reading, and writing
- Master Student Skills, including learning styles analysis, strategy training, and learning about the "culture" of U.S. colleges, which lead to their becoming successful students in degree courses and programs
- Topics and readings that represent a variety of academic disciplinary areas so that students learn about the language and content of the social sciences, the hard sciences, education, and business, as well as the humanities

All of the books provide . . .

- Interesting and valuable content that helps the students develop their knowledge of academic content as well as their language skills and student skills
- A wide variety of practical classroom-tested activities that are easy to teach and engage the students
- Assessment tools at the end of each chapter so that instructors have easy-to-implement ways to assess student learning and students have opportunities to assess their own growth
- Websites for students and instructors: the student sites will provide additional opportunities to practice reading, writing, listening, vocabulary development, and grammar. The instructor sites will provide instructors' manuals, teaching notes and answer keys, value-added materials like handouts and overheads that can be reproduced to use in class, and assessment tools such as additional tests to use beyond the assessment materials in each book

☐ What Is the Purpose of the Writing Strand?

The Writing strand of the Houghton Mifflin English for Academic Success series prepares ESL students for academic written work, particularly in the first two years of college study. Many ESL students have learned English mostly through their ears; others have studied English primarily with their eyes. Each group has unique written-language problems. The goals of the writing books are to build on the strengths of the students; to respect the knowledge they have; and to identify and teach language, content, and rhetoric that students must have to succeed in college courses. The writing strategies presented focus on confidence building and step-by-step, easy-to-learn processes for effective academic writing.

The four writing textbooks prepare students for the range of writing tasks assigned in college courses, and the solid scaffolding of skills focus on "college culture" as well as on academic writing. The high-interest content-based chapters relate to academic work and college disciplines, and the chapter materials have been designed to appeal to a variety of student learning styles and strategies. The authentic native-English, ESL, and professional writing samples offer students examples of required writing in post-secondary institutions; the writing assignments have been drawn from actual college courses across the curriculum. In addition, the content of each textbook is based on the Houghton Mifflin Writing Competencies, which in turn are based on state-designed competencies developed by hundreds of experienced ESL teachers.

Grammar and Technology in the Writing Strand

Because the ESL population is so diverse in its grammar and rhetoric needs, each chapter contains Power Grammar boxes that introduce structures needed by the students to write fluent, accurate academic prose. The structures are drawn from the writing required by the chapter content. Students who need additional work with the structures are referred to the Houghton Mifflin website, where high-quality relevant additional support is available.

Assignments in the writing textbooks also ask students to use the Internet: to investigate topics and to identify and evaluate sources for research. Materials about citing sources is sequenced and spiraled through the books so that students exit the writing program with substantial practice with and knowledge about using sources.

Assessment Materials Accompanying the Writing Strand

This Writing strand is filled with informal and formal assessment. Students write, self-assess, and have significant opportunities for peer response and other external informal review, including teacher response. The end of each chapter contains additional writing tasks for practice or for testing/evaluation. Each chapter also asks students to self-evaluate the skills they have learned; these self-evaluations have proven surprisingly honest and accurate, and the results allow teachers to review and recycle necessary concepts. Finally, students regularly return to the revision process.

More formally, the instructor website (http://esl.college.hmco.com/instructors) and *The Essentials of Teaching Academic Writing* book offer assessment information and advice about both responding to and "grading" student writing. Information in these sources helps instructors set up valid, reliable criteria for each student writing assignment in each book (which the instructors are encouraged to share with their students). These resources also contain sample student papers with teacher responses, sample topics to assess student strengths and weaknesses and to measure achievement and progress, and "benchmarked" student papers that describe the range of student grades.

Instructor Support Materials

The co-editors and Houghton Mifflin are committed to supporting instructors. For the Writing strand, the *Essentials of Teaching Academic Writing* by Joy Reid is an easily accessible, concise volume. This teacher resource, with its practical, problem-solving content, includes organizational suggestions for less experienced writing instructors, materials for response to and evaluation of student writing, and activities for teaching. In addition, each textbook has a password-protected website for instructors to provide classroom activities, substantial information and materials for assessment of student writing, and a "workbook" of printable pages linked to the textbook for use as handouts or overhead transparencies.

☐ What Is the Organization of *College Writing 4*?

College Writing 4, the final writing book in the Houghton Mifflin English for Academic Success series, transitions students from advanced English as a second language courses to genuine college work. Many students enrolled in this course will have had instruction in academic writing; others may have tested into a high level of ESL due to an overall fluency in English. The recursive approach taken in this text is designed to capitalize upon students' diverse backgrounds, interests, strengths, and learning styles—and to ensure their academic success.

The five research-based writing assignments mirror those that students will encounter in general education courses; in this way, students are exposed to a variety of college content areas and essay modes. They master important competencies in each chapter while following a sound, three-step writing process: gathering information; focusing and organizing; and drafting, revising, and editing. Students internalize these three steps to research writing as they move through the course and will certainly draw upon these skills in their future college and professional careers.

The course opens with a review of academic writing conventions. Students are then guided from objective, analytical reporting to evaluative, persuasive writing; the final assignment is a formal argumentative paper. Each of the five essay assignments requires students to narrow a topic and select credible sources to summarize, synthesize, and cite as they write their essays.

In Chapter 1, students select one Constitutional amendment to investigate and explain in its historical and/or current context. They conduct Internet searches and begin their writing with a background paragraph—a significant feature that may be new for many who have practiced the "five-paragraph essay" in prior courses.

In Chapter 2, students report on a communicable disease that has reached epidemic proportions in either present or past times. They begin their research on government websites provided in the text (e.g., CDC, WHO); they are also introduced to active reading and paraphrasing strategies that they will continue to build upon in subsequent chapters.

In Chapter 3, students identify characteristics of good learning environments and research how two of these features are accounted for in online courses. Students write a persuasive thesis and develop the essay with solid support based not only on readings in the field but also personal interviews with instructors and students involved in online learning.

In Chapter 4, students read local newspaper articles to select a controversial issue that currently affects their community. They investigate and report on both sides of a controversy in an objective manner, devoting equal emphasis to both *pros* and *cons*. If possible, students personally interview "experts," such as city officials, activists, and concerned residents who are involved in and/or affected by the issue. They incorporate direct quotations, paraphrases, and summaries from interviews and readings into their papers to fully explain both perspectives.

In Chapter 5, students add to what they have learned about outlining two sides of an argument and now take an argumentative stance on either the same local issue or another controversial topic. Students conduct surveys and incorporate results that support claims essential to their viewpoints. They choose strong evidence to refute the counterarguments of the opposition and organize the essay by choosing the most logical argumentative pattern of the three presented in the chapter.

Chapter Organization

Chapter Objectives

Each chapter begins with a preview of objectives that will aid students in completion of the writing assignment. After working through the chapter, students can assess their progress by returning to this list of goals and checking off the skills they have learned well and those they feel they still need practice with.

Self-Evaluation and Peer Reviews

Students are encouraged to read, discuss, and comment on the work of their peers as they move through the three-step writing process in each chapter. In this way, students share not only finished products but also their evolving ideas, supporting evidence, and methods of expression as they work through several drafts. Peer review sheets provided on both the instructor and student websites can be downloaded and used by students as a final checklist for their own papers as well as those of their classmates.

Power Grammar

Students review and practice select grammar points (e.g., writing definitions, qualifying opinions) that are integral to each chapter writing assignment. The "power" lies in the meaningful way these grammar exercises are linked to the chapter content and writing task. Interactive, self-correcting power grammar exercises on the student website extend the review and practice provided in each chapter. Instructors can also download brief quizzes from the instructor site to use for ongoing assessment as each chapter is completed.

Sample Essays

In each chapter, students analyze essays and parts of essays (e.g., introductions, body paragraphs) that have been written by previous students in response to the chapter writing assignments. These sample essays clearly illustrate academic writing skills (e.g., cohesion, development of ideas), concrete models of grammatical forms taught in power grammar sections, and topic-related concepts and vocabulary that are studied in the chapter.

Master Student Tips

Throughout *College Writing 4,* students receive advice, in the form of tips, on how best to approach or complete academic tasks. These tips are designed not only to help students through the writing assignment at hand but to lead them to successful academic careers.

Web Power

Students are guided through the process of conducting Internet searches to gather credible materials for their papers. They are also reminded that additional information and practice can be found on the accompanying Houghton Mifflin website.

Additional Practice and Resources

Each chapter ends with additional writing assignments for practice and assessment and reminds students to log on to the Houghton Mifflin website for more exercises. In addition to further practice with grammar and writing skills, the website also provides links to readings that familiarize students with academic discourse and help them build schema in content areas they are asked to research and write about.

Acknowledgments

Numerous people were involved in the creation of the Houghton Mifflin English for Academic Success series. The authors would like to express sincere thanks to the Houghton Mifflin team, in particular Susan Maguire and Kathy Sands Boehmer, for their belief in this project. With great respect, we thank the series editors Pat Byrd, Joy Reid, and Cynthia Schuemann; their knowledge is inspirational and their friendship cherished.

We would also like to express gratitude to many others who have shaped this book:

- ESL advisors who tested and critiqued materials, asked insightful questions, and offered ongoing support: Anne Decker, Sharon Donohue, and Susan Benson
- Specialists who visited classes and shared their expertise in disciplines related to chapter assignments: William Hale (journalism/freedom of the press), Dr. James Fozard (epidemiology), Gary Abernethy (distance education), Earl Fratus (government/Florida issues), and Herbert Hall (rehabilitative counseling/community activist)
- Reviewers at institutions across the country who offered valuable feedback at various stages during the creation of this book: Marsha Abramovich, Tidewater Community College; Jane Conzett, Zavier University; Julie Cheshire, Chemeketa Community College; Lynne Davis, Southern Illinois University; Patricia Juza, LaGuardia Community College; Robert Maguire, Boston University; Susan McQuerrey, Bakersfield College; Carole Miele, Bergen Community College; Brad Tucker, Georgia Perimeter College; and Will Zhang, Des Moines Area Community College
- Authors of *College Writing 1, 2,* and *3*: Karen Walsh, Eileen Cotter, and Gabriella Nuttall, who collaborated tirelessly to lend consistency to the scope of this series
- Writing strand editor Joy Reid, who brought an experienced, critical eye to every page and maintained a realistic focus while encouraging fresh ideas for each draft
- ESL students who worked hard through each lesson and chapter assignment, especially those whose work now appears in this book as learning tools for others

A heartfelt thanks goes to my co-author, Li-Lee Tunceren. Her warm personality was always apparent during this project, and her ideas helped to spark my own creativity. A special thanks also goes to my friend and colleague Debra Snell, whose encouragement and smiles carried me through. And finally, to my husband Alper and daughters Sera and Peri–I could not ask for stronger support. You are the joy of my life.

Sharon L. Cavusgil
Georgia State University
Atlanta, Georgia

I'd like to extend my sincere thanks to Sharon Cavusgil, whose ability to hone in on the essentials of academic writing contributed greatly to the selection and sequencing of material presented in this book. Her confidence and optimism carried us through many drafts. I must also thank my family, Vural, Emelle, Paul, and Joel, who have tolerated the priority this project has taken over many other activities and whose love and laughter keep me energized.

Li-Lee Tunceren
St. Petersburg College
Clearwater, Florida

☐ What Student Competencies Are Covered in *College Writing 4*?

Competency 1:
(level/global focus)

The student will demonstrate comprehension of academic writing tasks about general education content from a range of disciplines (i.e., academic cultures). (Text sources may include materials from Houghton Mifflin college "essentials" sources and college freshman level textbooks, as well as individual student-interest academic materials.)

Competency 2:
(flexibility)

The student will adjust writing strategies according to assignment and disciplinary demands, including varying overall and inner paragraph and essay organization to suit the writing task.

Competency 3:
(organization)

The student will produce variant forms of academic organization in writing assignments, including the use of synthesis, summary, background paragraphs, counterarguments, interpretation, and/or evaluation of texts, and the like that are expected in various disciplines (i.e., academic cultures).

Competency 4:
(research writing)

The student will select, evaluate, and appropriately use both primary and secondary research-based writing materials, including nontext materials and references, as well as using the structures and styles of disciplinary academic materials.

Competency 5:
(vocabulary)

The student will continue to develop disciplinary vocabulary by applying effective strategies to clarify, analyze, and use the new words.

Competency 6:
(organization)

The student will clarify and analyze the meaning of text for the disciplinary audience through such writing strategies as outlining, paraphrasing, and summarizing, providing textual clues, and using and citing sources.

Competency 7:
(grammar)

The student will write accurate Standard English appropriate to the discipline and writing assignments, including proofreading and editing grammar and sentence structure appropriate to the level.

Competency 8:
(critical thinking)

The student will apply the following critical thinking skills through writing: develop and practice additional skills and strategies for analysis of academic writing tasks, academic audiences, and academic purposes; develop perspectives and practice a sense of "voice" through the exploration of beliefs, arguments, and theories; clarify understanding of issues raised in primary and secondary source materials through the use of specific detail; articulate plausible and persuasive implications or consequences; generate and assess solutions persuasively; apply knowledge gained from reading and writing to other contexts and academic tasks (e.g., discussion, authentic academic writing assignments, test taking, academic interactions).

Competency 9:
(culture)

The student will demonstrate familiarity with common cultural schema.

Competency 10:
(study strategies)

The student will continue and expand the effective use of study skills, learning styles, and strategies necessary when writing for academic purposes.

☐ What Are the Features of the Writing Books?

The Houghton Mifflin English for Academic Success series is a comprehensive program of student and instructor materials. The fundamental purpose of the program is to prepare students who are not native speakers of English for academic success in U.S. college degree programs.

The Writing strand of the Houghton Mifflin English for Academic Success series focuses on the development of writing skills and general background knowledge necessary for college study. The series is dedicated to meeting academic needs of students by teaching them how to handle the writing demands and expectations of college-level classes. The goals of the writing books are to build on the strengths of the students; to respect the knowledge they have; and to identify and teach language, content, and rhetoric that students must have to succeed in college courses.

Academic Content: The content of each book relates to academic subjects and has been selected because of its high interest for students and because of the popularity of these particular disciplines/courses on college campuses.

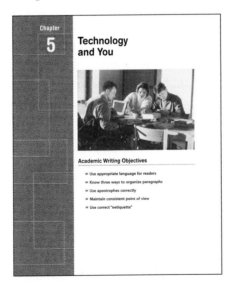

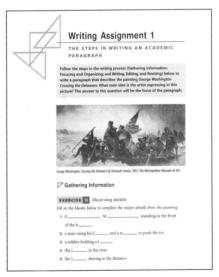

Authentic Writing Assignments: The writing assignments have been drawn from actual college courses across the curriculum. Students will find the assignments highly motivating when they realize they may receive such an assignment in one of their future classes.

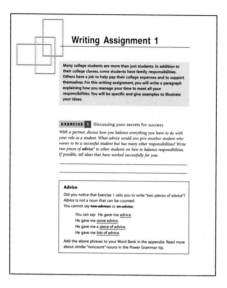

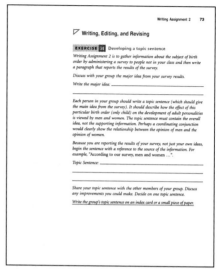

Authentic Writing Models: Models provide specific examples of student writing so that students can compare writing styles, discuss writing strategies, and understand instructor expectations.

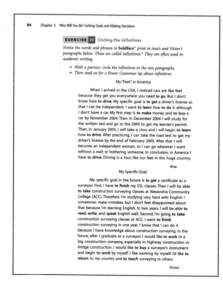

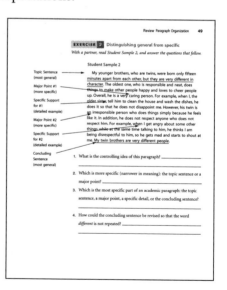

Step-by-Step Writing Process: The step-by-step writing process helps demystify the concept of "academic writing" and helps students develop confidence. The textbooks offer solid scaffolding of skills that focus on college culture as well as on academic topics and academic writing. These are supplemented by practical advice offered in the Spotlight on Writing Skills feature boxes.

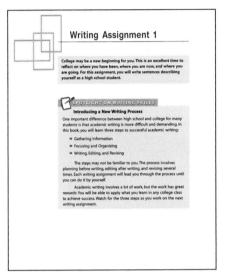

Self-Assessment Opportunity: A writing course develops through assessment. Students write and revise and instructors respond and evaluate and then students write some more. The textbooks offer students opportunity for peer review, self-review, and self-evaluation.

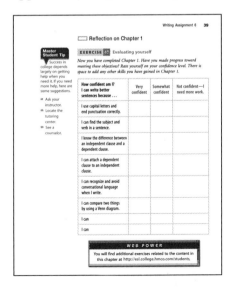

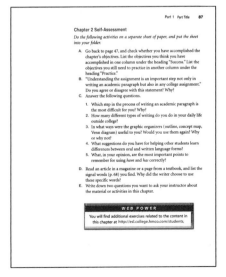

Master Student Tips: Master Student Tips throughout the textbooks provide students with short comments on a particular strategy, activity, or practical advice to follow in an academic setting.

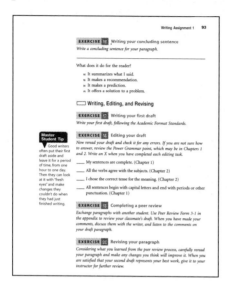
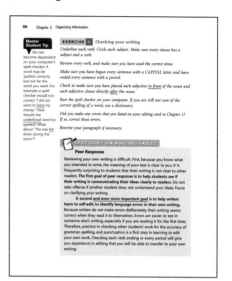

Power Grammar Boxes: Students can be very diverse in their grammar and rhetorical needs, so each chapter contains Power Grammar boxes that introduce the grammar structures students need to be fluent and accurate in academic English.

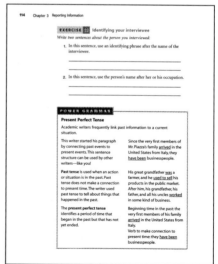

Ancillary Program: The ancillary program provides instructors with teaching tips, additional exercises, and robust assessment. Students can also take advantage of additional exercises and activities. The following items are available to accompany the Houghton Mifflin English for Academic Success series Writing strand.

- Instructor website: Additional teaching materials, activities, and robust student assessment.
- Student website: Additional exercises, activities, and web links.
- The Houghton Mifflin English for Academic Success series Vocabulary books. You can choose the appropriate level to shrink-wrap with your text.
- The *Essentials of Teaching Academic Writing* by Joy M. Reid is available for purchase. It gives you theoretical and practical information for teaching academic writing.

Writing an Expository Essay

Most academic writing is *expository*. That is, the writer's purpose is to explain ideas and events by:

- **Investigating**
- **Describing what, how, and/or why something takes place**
- **Illustrating those explanations by providing facts, examples, description, and/or experience**

Chapter Objectives

Read the following chapter objectives to preview the chapter content. After you complete the chapter, return to this chart and check (✓) the appropriate boxes on the right.	I have learned this well.	I need to work on this.
Follow a three-step writing process to gather, organize, and draft information		
Read and mark ideas and details in academic materials		
Search the Internet for source information		
Learn the conventions of academic writing		
Understand the importance of audience and purpose		
Construct an information chart to synthesize information		
Understand expository essay development		
Create an essay map to organize information		
Write effective thesis statements		
Use cohesion devices to connect ideas		
Cite sources within your essay		
Use non-restrictive relative clauses and appositives to establish expert credibility		
Draft an end-of-text reference list		

Chapter Writing Assignment

You will research one U.S. Constitutional amendment (or one aspect of an amendment) to explain its meaning in a three- to four-page expository essay. Your essay must include the following:

- An introductory paragraph
- A background paragraph that includes factual and/or historical information about the amendment
- Two or three body paragraphs that explain the meaning of the amendment
- A concluding paragraph
- At least two to four in-text citations
- An end-of-text reference page with references for all sources referred to as you wrote your essay

Throughout this book, you will complete writing assignments, like this chapter's expository essay, following a three-step writing process:

1. Gathering Information
2. Focusing and Organizing
3. Drafting, Revising, and Editing

☐ Gathering Information

Gathering information about a topic from various sources helps you complete expository essays and other academic writing assignments. Class discussions, reading, and other exercises in this chapter will help you gather, organize, and select ideas for this chapter's writing assignment.

EXERCISE 1 Discussing the U.S. Constitution

Review the opening illustration for this chapter, and read this passage about the U.S. Constitution. Then, discuss answers to the following questions with your classmates and instructor. You are not expected to know all the answers yet. You will learn much more about the subject as you work through this chapter.

The U.S. Constitution

The United States Constitution, written in 1787, states the laws and rules by which the country is governed. These laws and rules are outlined in the Constitution as amendments. Currently, the U.S. Constitution has 27 amendments. These amendments explain the rights guaranteed to all citizens. For example, the First Amendment, which ensures that U.S. citizens have the freedom of religion, speech, press, assembly, and petition, states:

> Congress shall make no law respecting an establishment of religion or prohibiting the free exercise thereof; or abridging the freedom of speech, or of the press; or the right of the people peaceably to assemble, and to petition the Government for a redress of grievances.

The first ten amendments are known as the Bill of Rights. The Bill of Rights includes such laws as "the right to bear arms" (The Second Amendment) and "the right to remain silent" (one aspect of the Fifth Amendment).

(You can also visit the Houghton Mifflin website at http://esl.college.hmco.com/students to read more about the Bill of Rights.)

1. In what century was the U.S. Constitution written?
2. Name one or two writers of the Constitution.
3. Name two or three rights the Constitution guarantees all U.S. citizens.
4. Why do you think it is important to have a Constitution and Bill of Rights?

EXERCISE 2   **Writing about the U.S. Constitution**

This exercise will give your instructor an introduction to your writing style. Write your reaction to one of the following questions. When you finish, review your writing and make any necessary changes and corrections.

1. Why do you think it is important to have a Constitution and Bill of Rights?
2. How does the Bill of Rights affect our daily lives?
3. Which amendment or basic right interests you the most? Why?

SPOTLIGHT ON WRITING SKILLS

Conventions of Academic Writing

Expository writing, like all academic writing, typically follows certain "rules," or *conventions*, about the organization and presentation of written material. These rules are called conventions because they are conventional (typical) practices that readers expect. Understanding these conventions can help you do well on college writing and reading assignments.

For example, readers expect an academic paragraph to have three parts:
1. Topic sentence (including a topic and controlling ideas)
2. Supporting information (main points and details)
3. Concluding sentence

Topic Sentences

Topic sentences help writers keep their ideas focused, and they help readers understand what the paragraph is about. The *topic sentence* is a general statement that states the main idea of a paragraph. The topic sentence does not have to be the first sentence of a paragraph. However, placing the topic sentence at the beginning of a paragraph helps the reader identify the focus of the writing.

The *controlling ideas* in the topic sentence are words and phrases that direct and control the paragraph. They tell the readers what will be developed in the paragraph. Readers often ask questions about the controlling ideas that they expect will be answered in the paragraph. These questions can include *who? what? where? when? why? how?* and *how much?* Writers should try to answer some of these questions when developing their paragraphs.

Supporting Information

An academic paragraph contains a topic sentence and supporting information. *Supporting information* includes specific details that support, explain, or prove the general claim or statement made in the topic sentence. Writers can support general claims or statements by including one or more of the following in their paragraphs:

- Facts or statistics
- Expert opinions
- Descriptions
- Explanations
- Examples
- Personal experiences
- Observations

When writers include supporting information in their paragraphs, they are *developing their ideas.*

EXERCISE 3 **Analyzing academic writing conventions**

Review academic conventions by following these steps:

1. Read the paragraph and comments in the margin.
2. Draw lines to connect the comments to the appropriate sections in the paragraph.
3. Complete the outline that follows the paragraph.
4. Discuss your ideas about academic writing conventions with your classmates and instructor.

Student Paragraph: The First Amendment

The introductory sentence presents the topic.

The topic sentence includes the topic and controlling ideas of the paragraph.

The paragraph first focuses on government limitations.

An example is introduced with a logical organizer (*For example*). See Appendix 4 for a list.

Specific details explain the example.

The focus changes to individual rights, signaled with a logical organizer (*likewise*).

An example is introduced with a logical organizer.

The paragraph concludes with the significance of the decision.

The First Amendment lists several fundamental freedoms for Americans, beginning with the important Establishment Clause: "Congress shall make no law respecting an establishment of religion. . ." (The Legal Information, n.d., para. 3). In other words, the establishment clause of the First Amendment states that the government cannot promote religious activities and individuals must be allowed to practice religion as they wish. Public schools in the United States are often the focus of this clause. Because public schools are extensions of the government, by law, children cannot be requested to say a prayer in the morning or even the Pledge of Allegiance to the flag. This would mean that the government encourages religious behavior, which would be unconstitutional. For example, in one case taken to the Supreme Court, the Court ruled that school children cannot be made to show patriotism if that is against their religious beliefs. The decision came after two students, Jehovah's Witnesses, were suspended from school for refusing to salute the American flag or recite the Pledge of Allegiance. Their parents and attorneys maintained that showing reverence to any symbol constituted idolatry, which violated their religious laws (Monk, 1995). Likewise, students can practice religion as they wish. If a student is absent to observe a religious holy day, the school cannot penalize the child. For instance, the teacher cannot give a zero on a test but instead must make arrangements for the child to take the exam on another day. Another Supreme Court case illustrates this clause. In 1972, a Supreme Court decision exempted Amish people living in Wisconsin from that state's compulsory school attendance law (Monk, 1995). In both Supreme Court cases, the Court respected these individuals' rights to act according to their beliefs and required the state to practice tolerance of diverse religions.

The first source does not include an author, so it is alphabetized by the organization name.

A period is not used at the end of the Internet address.

The second source is alphabetized by the author's last name (Monk).

References

The Legal Information Institute. (n.d.) *The Constitution of the United States*. Retrieved May 12, 2004, from http://www.law.cornell.edu/constitution/constitution.overview.html

Monk, L. (1995). *The First Amendment: America's blueprint for tolerance*. Washington, D.C.: Close Up Foundation Publication.

Outline for Student Paragraph: The First Amendment

Topic Sentence:

_____

_____

_____

Main Point 1:   The government cannot promote religious activities.
Supporting Information:

_____

_____

_____

Main Point 2:   Individuals must be allowed to practice religion as they wish.
Supporting Information:

_____

_____

_____

Concluding Sentence:

_____

_____

Citing Outside Sources

Many academic assignments require students to refer to and explain their understanding of information located in other sources (e.g., websites, textbooks, newspapers). When you include information from outside sources in your paper, you must let your readers know where this information came from. In other words, you must cite sources. When you cite,

   a. Include the name(s) of the author(s) whose ideas and words you used in your paper,

   b. Include the year of publication and other important information.

   In addition, on a separate page,

   c. Include a list of

- Any work that influenced your writing and
- Any work that you included in your paper.

Different academic disciplines use different systems to cite sources. The APA (American Psychological Association) style is commonly used by the social sciences (e.g., economics, psychology, political science). The MLA (Modern Language Association) style is often used in humanities courses, like literature or history. This textbook focuses on the APA style.

Example In-text Citation (APA style):

At the Constitutional Convention in Philadelphia, George Washington suggested adding a list of civil liberties, called the Bills of Rights (Janda, Berry, & Goldman, 2002).

(last names of multiple authors, year of publication) included in parentheses.

Example End-of-Text Reference (APA style):

names of multiple authors   (year of publication).   book title
Janda, K., Berry, J., & Goldman, J. (2002). *The challenge of*

(edition).   location: publisher.
democracy (7th ed.). Boston: Houghton Mifflin.

(See Appendixes 1–3 for more information on citation.)

EXERCISE 4   Searching the Internet

You have already begun to gather information by discussing, writing, and reading about amendments of the U.S. Constitution. Continue to gather information by visiting the Houghton Mifflin website at http://esl.college.hmco.com/students.

1. At the Houghton Mifflin website, click on the link to this book, Chapter 1.
2. Locate information about the Bill of Rights (the first ten amendments) and *skim*—read quickly without making notes. You might also want to skim other amendments, like the Fourteenth Amendment, which grants equal rights to all U.S. citizens, and the Nineteenth Amendment, which grants women the right to vote.
3. Do not worry if you cannot understand the amendments completely. Use this first reading to become familiar with the formal language used and the basic rights granted in the amendments.
4. Print a copy of the amendments that interest you.
5. In your academic papers, you will need to include citation information, so on each document you print, record the website's URL (address), the date you printed the document, and other information that is provided like the author, title, and date of publication.

Examples:

    author   (date published)   article title   newspaper

a. Ashe, K. (2003, January 10). Our rights. *Los Angeles Times*.

    date info was printed   website's URL
    Retrieved January 21, 2005, from http://www.latimes.com

    website's URL

b. http://www.cornell.edu/constitution/constitution.billofrights.
        date info was printed
    html. Retrieved December 31, 2004. (*Note*: An author, title, and date of publication were not provided.)

EXERCISE 5 **Reading and taking notes about amendments**

Parts of the Constitution may be difficult to understand. One reason is that the document was written more than 200 years ago, and language has changed to include new words and eliminate others. Also, the writing style of the Constitution is very formal and meant for legal purposes, so it is not surprising if you feel confused when reading about amendments. Reading to locate specific information may help.

1. Reread the documents you located about amendments and their explanations. Look for information that explains
   a. the meaning of each of these amendments
   b. the purpose of each amendment. Was the amendment written to:

      ■ protect individual rights?
      ■ make public policy?
      ■ correct deficiencies in the government's structure?
      ■ promote equality?

   c. the significance of these amendments. In other words, why is each amendment important and what could happen if the amendment did not exist?

2. Take notes of important information in the margins of the documents and/or highlight or underline this information.

EXERCISE 6 **Discussing and selecting amendments**

Discussing the amendments with others may also help you better understand the information.

1. Form small groups, and choose three amendments that interest your group members. In your groups,
   a. discuss the meaning of each of those amendments
   b. decide the purpose of each amendment
   c. discuss the significance of these amendments

2. Select one of these three amendments to study for this chapter's writing assignment. Group members do not need to select the same amendment. Write your selection here:

   _____

   _____

EXERCISE **7** **Writing about your amendment**

Write about your chosen amendment:

> **Master Student Tip**
>
> Freewriting helps you understand what you know and do not know about a topic. Freewriting also helps you get your ideas on paper.

1. For five minutes, freewrite about the purpose of your chosen amendment or its significance. You may include:

   ■ Some of the ideas discussed with your group members in the previous exercise

   ■ Information from your readings

   ■ Ideas from personal experiences and knowledge you have about the rights of people in the United States or other nations

   When you write, do not be concerned about grammar, spelling, or punctuation. Do not worry about the appropriateness or organization of your ideas or your vocabulary choice.

2. When the time limit is up, spend another five minutes reviewing your writing and adding to or changing your ideas. Place your writing in your notebook or folder for future reference.

☐ Focusing and Organizing

In the first step of the writing process, you gathered information by discussing, writing, and reading. In the second step, you will focus and organize your materials in preparation for writing your paper.

SPOTLIGHT ON WRITING SKILLS

Audience and Purpose

Always write for a particular *audience*, a group of readers with common characteristics. When you identify your audience/readers, you can predict their expectations and fulfill those expectations in your writing. Also, have a clear understanding of the *purpose* of your writing—what you are trying to achieve (e.g., educate, persuade, demonstrate your knowledge). When you understand your audience and purpose, you can better plan what material to introduce and how to effectively present this information.

To analyze your audience and purpose and to help you further plan your writing assignment, answer the following questions:

1. Who are my readers? Their age? Gender? Level of education?
2. Why will they read my essay?
3. What do they already know about my topic?
4. What don't they know?
5. What do I want to communicate to them?
6. How can I best present that information to them?

EXERCISE 8   **Understanding audience and purpose**

> **Master Student Tip**
> For most college writing, your *audience* is your instructor and perhaps your classmates. Your *purpose* is to demonstrate your understanding of the subject matter you are studying.

Understand audience and purpose by completing the following:

1. Study one student's answers to the previous questions about her audience and purpose. This student's analysis of her audience and purpose served as a valuable guide for her writing.

    a. <u>Who are my readers?</u> my instructor and classmates; aged 25–45; mixed genders; college degree or in college

    b. <u>Why will they read my essay?</u> Instructor—to assess my understanding of the conventions of academic writing; to see if I understand the First Amendment. Classmates—to learn about the First Amendment and its effects in history and today; to learn more vocabulary related to this subject; to analyze conventions of writing; to compare their essays to mine

    c. <u>What do they already know about my topic?</u> some general ideas from life, the news, movies, and books; as much as I knew before I started to research the amendment

    d. <u>What don't they know?</u> not much about the language used or why the amendment was proposed; no names or dates of famous cases; what's usually accepted/what's controversial

    e. <u>What do I want to communicate to them?</u> I want them to:

    • Realize how often the 1st amendment is used, especially about freedom of religion in the U.S.
    • Learn how much interpretation is necessary and how time periods can change judges' opinions
    • See that not everyone agrees on all freedoms
    • See that this is interesting information and a significant part of a democratic government that maybe they didn't think about before reading my paper

f. <u>How can I best present that information to them?</u> I need to:
- Define some terms
- Emphasize the strong language/the way it was written
- Show how much the amendment applies to daily life
- Show some examples where judges have disagreed and people have protested after a decision
- Find recent reports to prove its current/ongoing interpretation when society changes

2. For your own topic, write responses to questions a–f listed previously. Think of these responses as a way to help you select appropriate, interesting material for your essay and present it in a manner that fulfills your readers' expectations.

3. Share your responses with two or three of your classmates and/or instructor. If your classmates have thought of other responses that will help guide your writing, add those ideas to your list.

SPOTLIGHT ON WRITING SKILLS

Information Charts to Synthesize Ideas

As a writer, you will always gather more information than you will use. From your information, you select the ideas, supporting details, and examples that (a) communicate your information and ideas to your readers and (b) interest your readers.

One effective way to collect and select material for your essay is to construct an *information chart* to help you visualize main ideas and supporting details. Information in the chart is taken from a variety of sources, so you can examine similarities and differences in reports by various authors. When you select information from several sources and combine that information with your own ideas, you are *synthesizing*— an essential academic skill. Equally important, an information chart includes the source of materials you gathered for your paper. Knowing the source of these materials is crucial because you must cite sources when you use others' ideas in your academic writing.

The following sample is a student's first experience with an information chart. It contains entries from only two sources. As you continue to gather information for your expository essay, your own chart will grow much longer.

Information Chart: Essay on the First Amendment

Authors (credentials)	Sources (for in-text citation & reference page)	Main Points & Quotations	Supporting Details
Linda Monk: Newspaper writer, Harvard Law grad., won American Bar Assoc's Gavel Award	(book) Monk, L. (1995). The first Amendment: America's blueprint for tolerance. Washington D.C.: Close Up Foundation Publication.	First Amendment = tolerance of diverse lifestyles (p. 20) Citizens challenging state laws has led to Supreme Court cases & different decisions over the yrs. (p. 36)	School policies: saluting flag, prayer, banned books (p. 36) Free press ex. —Sedition Act (p. 51) —Near vs. Minnesota (p. 62) —Pentagon Papers
Horst Pottker, German journalist/media expert & Kenneth Starck, Prof, Univ of Iowa, School of Journalism and Mass Comm.	(online journal) Pottker, H. & Starck, K. (2003). Criss-crossing perspectives: Contrasting models of press self-regulation in Germany and the United States. Journalism Studies, Vol. 4 Issue 1, p. 47. Rutledge, Ltd. Retrieved Dec 22, 2003, from http://search.epnet.com/direct.asp	Freedom = social respons. More "press responsibility" needed in U.S. than reporters have now. Instead, reporters often > responsive to public opinions/demands (p. 32)	Freedom & responsibilities are dueling . . . (p. 49) Hutchin's report: relative power of press = obligations (p. 50)

EXERCISE 9 Constructing an information chart

Construct an information chart like the previous example.

1. Make four columns, and title them (a) Authors, (b) Sources, (c) Main Points & Quotations, and (d) Supporting Details.

2. Review the readings you have located so far, and fill in the chart.

    - When completing the *Authors* column, include information (e.g., academic degrees, professional positions) that will help you explain why the author is credible.
    - Include terms you need to define in order to explain or understand your topic.
    - Include supporting information (like facts, examples) you might use in your paper.
    - Write only keywords and phrases that will remind you about the ideas.
    - Include only a few direct quotations; it is best to try to put others' ideas into your own words (paraphrase).
    - Include page numbers of the original sources so that you can return to those pages if needed.

3. Share your chart with a classmate. If possible, work with a classmate who is writing on the same topic. Together, decide if your charts include:

    - Complete credential information
    - Valid credentials (e.g., education, experience)
    - Up-to-date sources
    - Main ideas with page numbers
    - Quotations with page numbers
    - Supporting details with page numbers.

    Add ideas from your classmate's chart that may help you with your paper.

4. Review the writing assignment at the beginning of the chapter, and decide if you need to locate additional sources to fully develop your ideas. If so, talk with your instructor about possible additional sources.

5. Save your chart in your notebook or folder. Your instructor may want to collect a copy of your chart for review or evaluation.

SPOTLIGHT ON WRITING SKILLS

Essay Development for Expository Essays

Many college assignments, including this chapter's writing assignment, require you to write a multiple-page essay. Following is a chart of the overall organization of academic expository essays.

Chart: Organization of Expository Essays

Introductory Paragraph

- Stimulate your readers' interest in your topic.
- Provide brief information (about one to four sentences) about the topic.
- Include a clear thesis statement that explains the focus of your paper.

Background Paragraph

- Include information that is factual and/or historical, explaining the background of the topic that readers need.
- Ask yourself information questions, like *who? what? when? where? why?* and *how?* Responses to these questions and citations of sources where you found the answers may be included in your background paragraph.

Body Paragraphs (Usually two to six paragraphs for most assignments)

For each body paragraph,
- Begin with a topic sentence that relates directly to the thesis statement and contains both a main idea and controlling idea(s).
- Illustrate the major ideas with specific examples and details.
- Use logical organizers to show the relationship between ideas.
- Include in-text citation for any sources used.
- End with a brief concluding sentence.

Concluding Paragraph

- Remind readers of the main points developed in your essay.
- Relate the conclusion to remarks in the introduction.
- Provide the reader with final comments on the topic.
- Do not introduce more information or a new angle on the topic.

End-of-Text Reference Page

On a separate page, list all the sources referred to when you wrote your paper. (See Appendix 3, "End-of-Text References," for more details.)

EXERCISE 10 Identifying the parts of an expository essay

Review the conventions of academic writing, including the development of an expository essay, by reading this student essay and the comments in the margin. Draw lines to connect the comments to the appropriate sections in the essay. Then, with a partner, answer the questions that follow.

Student Essay: Separation of Church and State

The introduction includes a general statement and brief info about the topic.

The thesis statement includes the topic and controlling ideas.

The background paragraph includes historical info.

A quote with the ellipsis mark (…) is included. This indicates the writer omitted words unnecessary for this paper.

The paragraph includes a topic sentence and controlling ideas focusing on "importance" and "controversy."

The First Amendment to the U.S. Constitution allows people in the United States to practice any or no religion, to express their opinions in public, to investigate and write about people and events, to hold meetings to discuss their beliefs, and to protest against government policies (Monk, 1995). An examination of the First Amendment reveals a complex set of laws written to restrict the power of the government and protect the rights of citizens. The freedom of religion, one component of the First Amendment, is an important yet controversial liberty.

In 1787, the writers of the Constitution worked to design a government that would grant power at both federal and state levels, but their initial document did not include a list of civil rights for the people. In response, at the Constitutional Convention in Philadelphia, George Washington suggested adding a list of civil liberties, called the Bill of Rights (Janda, Berry, & Goldman, 2003; Monk, 1995). Thus, the First Amendment of the Bill of Rights begins with powerful phrases: "Congress shall make no law respecting an establishment of religion, or prohibiting the free exercise thereof . . . or the right of the people peaceably to assemble. . ." (The Legal Information, n.d., para. 3). In simple English, the First Amendment states that the government cannot tell people what to believe. In particular, regarding religion, there is a "separation of church and state." The government cannot interfere in religious issues, whether to encourage or prohibit any type of worship (Monk, 1995).

One reason the First Amendment is important is that a society with many different religions can face tense situations. For example, when students of various religious faiths attend

This general claim is supported with an example.

Sentences with specific details support the idea of "conflicts due to religious beliefs."

In-text citation with page # of direct quote are included.

public schools, there can be conflicts due to specific beliefs. During World War II, for instance, two children were suspended from school for refusing to salute the American flag because their religious beliefs did not allow allegiance to anything except God. Their family sued the Virginia State Board of Education. The Supreme Court decided that individual religious beliefs were fundamental to the First Amendment and that "patriotism should be voluntary" (Monk, 1995, p. 29). The issue of school prayer has also caused much debate in the United States. Schools are government agencies, so even if the majority of parents voted for a morning prayer, this practice would remain unconstitutional. In fact, the Supreme Court ruled in 1985 that not just prayer but even a daily moment of silence would "describe prayer as a favored practice" (Monk, 1995, p. 23). The First Amendment prohibits the government from promoting any such preference for religious behavior.

The topic sentence with controlling ideas explain the focus of the second body paragraph.

The general claim is supported with an example.

Sentences with specific details illustrate the controlling idea.

Generally, the government cannot interfere with religious beliefs. However, when a religious practice could interfere with public safety, the government may have to intervene. To illustrate, in Florida, Sultaana Freeman, a 35-year-old woman who practices Islam, always wears her niqab (a veil) in public. According to a CNN Student News Report (2003), when Freeman was told to remove the niqab for her Florida driver's license photo, she refused and sued the state highway department for violating her right to express her religious beliefs. In a Florida court, however, Freeman lost her case against the government. According to Judy Thorpe, the judge who oversaw this case, if Freeman wanted to drive in Florida, she would have to follow state rules (Branom, 2003). The judge added that one picture of Freeman's face for identification purposes would not affect her freedom to practice her religion. She further explained that the state "has a compelling interest in protecting the public from criminal activities and security threats," and that photo identification "is essential to promote that interest" (Branom, 2003). It is clear from this case how complicated interpreting First Amendment rights becomes in practical situations.

The paragraph ends with a brief concluding sentence.

The First Amendment is an essential legal guarantee in this diverse country, and citizens have the right to seek justice when their individual rights have been violated.

The conclusion reminds readers of the main points.

Final comments conclude the essay.

Reference information for sources is listed on a separate page.

See Appendix 3, "End-of-Text References," for more information.

Americans who value freedom and democracy owe much to the progressive thinkers who framed the Constitution and the First Amendment. Without their insight and dedication, the United States government and its people could not have maintained all the liberties that citizens enjoy today.

References

Branom, M. (2003, June 6). *Judge: Woman can't wear veil in ID photo*, Associated Press. Retrieved January 21, 2005, from the Mercury News Website: http://www.bayarea.com/mldbayarea/news/6030399.htm

CNN Student News. (2003, May 29). *Woman sues Florida over driver's license dispute*. Retrieved January 22, 2005, from the CNN Student News Website: http://us.cnn.com/2003/fyi/news/05/29/license.veil

Janda, K., Berry, J., & Goldman, J. (2002). *The challenge of democracy* (7th ed.). Boston: Houghton Mifflin.

The Legal Information Institute. (n.d.) *The Constitution of the United States*. Retrieved May 12, 2004, from http://www.law.cornell.edu/constitution/constitution.overview.html

Monk, L. (1995). *The First Amendment: America's blueprint for tolerance*. Washington, DC: Close Up Foundation Publishing.

1. In the margin of this essay, label each paragraph (e.g., introductory, background).Use the essay chart on page 18 as a guide.
2. Reread the thesis statement. Write three or four questions you expect to be answered in the essay.
3. Without rereading the essay, make a list of two to three details (supporting information) that you remember from the essay.
4. Look for the answers to your questions from #2. Does the essay answer all/most/some of your questions? Label the answers by highlighting or underlining them in the essay.
5. Circle uses of in-text citation in the essay. How many citations are included in this essay? _____

SPOTLIGHT ON WRITING SKILLS

Cohesion

Effective academic writers help their readers by using *cohesion devices,* writing techniques that:

- Help the parts of an essay "stick together"
- Signal the relationship between the parts of an essay

There are various cohesion devices that make ideas easy to read and understand.

1. Generally, *the government* cannot interfere with *religious beliefs*. However, if a *religious practice* interferes with public safety, *the government* may need to intervene.	Repetition of keywords and phrases
2. *If* a student is absent to observe a religious holy day, the school cannot penalize the child. *For instance,* the teacher cannot give a zero on a test, *but* instead must make arrangements for the child to take the exam on another day.	Logical organizers
3. Congress had to *propose* another amendment in 1933 to repeal the Eighteenth Amendment. *This proposal* outlined why the amendment should be ratified.	Different forms of a word
4. *The writers of the Constitution* realized that this document would have to be changed from time to time. To this end, *they* specified a formal amendment process that has two stages: proposal and ratification.	Pronouns

EXERCISE **11** Identifying cohesion devices

In the previous student essay, identify one or two examples of each type of cohesion device. In the margin next to each example of cohesion, include these abbreviations:

- Rep = Repetition of keywords and phrases
- L.O. =Logical organizers
- Wd Fm = Different forms of a word
- Pro = Pronouns

SPOTLIGHT ON WRITING SKILLS

Thesis Statements

A *thesis statement* states the main idea of an entire essay. It is a guide for the development of your topic. The thesis statement:

- Normally occurs at the end of the introductory paragraph
- Governs what material is included in the essay
- Shows how that information will be arranged

A thesis statement includes *a topic* and *controlling ideas* that direct and control the entire essay. (A topic sentence states the main idea of only one paragraph.)

EXERCISE **12** Understanding thesis statements

To help you better understand thesis statements, follow these steps:

1. With a partner, read the following thesis statements. For each statement, underline the topic and circle the controlling idea(s).
2. Discuss the meaning of each amendment (i.e., the topic).
3. Write two or three questions related to the controlling ideas that a writer could answer in the body paragraphs.
4. For each thesis statement, write a topic sentence that could be used for one of the essay's body paragraphs.

Example:

Thesis Statement:

<u>Freedom of religion</u> (one aspect of the First Amendment) is

(highly valued) in the United States, but this freedom

(can cause problems) in (our schools) and in (the workplace).

Questions about the Topic:

Why is this freedom so highly valued in the United States?
What problems occur in our schools?
How can these problems be reduced or eliminated?

Topic Sentence:
The various religious beliefs in the United States can cause tension in the school systems.

1. Thesis Statement: The Fifth Amendment protects civil liberties prized by a democratic society that values personal freedom.

Questions about the Topic:

_____

_____

_____

_____

Topic Sentence:

_____

_____

2. Thesis Statement: For several reasons, the Second Amendment is perhaps the most essential amendment in the Bill of Rights.

Questions about the Topic:

_____

_____

_____

_____

Topic Sentence:

_____

_____

3. Thesis Statement: This paper illustrates various ways the guarantees of the Fourteenth Amendment are upheld in educational institutions, in the workplace, and in lifestyle choices.

Questions about the Topic:

_____

_____

_____

_____

_____

_____

Topic Sentence:

_____

_____

SPOTLIGHT ON WRITING SKILLS

Essay Maps

An _essay map_ is an outline of the parts of your essay, along with the ideas you plan to include in each section. An essay map is an organizational tool that helps you to visualize your entire essay. It helps you draft a cohesive paper because you see clearly how the ideas in your thesis statement are (or are not) connected to the ideas in your topic sentences.

You will probably revise your essay map several times before you finish your final paper. Therefore, consider your essay map a "work-in-progress" that is always open to improvement.

Essay Map: Paper on the First Amendment

<u>Introductory Paragraph</u>	Include a quote about 1st amendment, basic info about amendment, and thesis statement.
Thesis Statement:	One of the most (valued) yet (controversial) (liberties) guaranteed by the 1st amendment is the (freedom of religion).
<u>Background Paragraph</u> Topic Sentence:	The original writers of the amendment wanted to protect people from the government— (value of freedom)
Questions to be answered in the paragraph:	Why did they want to "protect" people? How did they protect people's rights? How effective is the amendment?
Support:	historical info (before, people were unable to practice as desired), info about how they accomplished their goal
<u>Body Paragraph 1</u> Topic Sentence:	Different religious expressions can cause (problems/tension) in society, e.g., public schools (prayers, attendance)
Questions to be answered in the paragraph:	What different religious beliefs/practices exist in the U.S.? How/why do they cause tension? What can be done to eliminate/reduce tension?
Support:	WWII—students refusing to salute flag (families sued) Supreme Court ruling against school prayers

Body Paragraph 2 Topic Sentence: Questions to be answered in the paragraph:	The government (cannot interfere with religious) beliefs What is meant by "interfering?" Why happens if the government does interfere? Are there examples to illustrate this?
Support:	driver's license photo (Freeman)
Concluding Paragraph	remind readers of main point—essential legal guarantee final comments (praising men who drafted Constitution)

EXERCISE 13 **Drafting a thesis statement and essay map**

To draft a thesis statement and essay map for your paper, follow these steps:

1. Reread the chapter writing assignment.
2. Take out the readings you gathered on your amendment, your information chart, and any writing you completed so far. Review this material for ideas and support for your essay.
3. Draft a "working" thesis statement that includes the main idea and controlling ideas that you plan to develop in your essay.
4. Create an essay map by listing the components of the essay on the left side of a sheet of paper, as you saw in the previous example. On the right side, complete the essay map with your plans to develop the essay. Specifically, fill in:

- Your working thesis statement
- Background information you expect your readers need
- A topic sentence for each body paragraph that relates to a controlling idea in the thesis
- Major points and supporting information to support the topic sentences
- Idea(s) you want to emphasize in your conclusion

SPOTLIGHT ON WRITING SKILLS

Citing Sources

To include information from outside sources in your paper, you can:

a. *Quote* the ideas (copy them exactly and put quotation marks around them) or

b. *Paraphrase* the ideas (write them in your own words).

With both quoting and paraphrasing, you must incorporate *in-text citation*. When you use in-text citation, you include the author's name and the author's ideas in your paper. See Appendixes 1–2 for more information. Chapter 2, page 81, also discusses quoting and paraphrasing in more detail.

☐ Drafting, Revising, and Editing

You have gathered information about your topic and focused and organized your materials in preparation for this chapter's writing assignment. The third step of the writing process includes:

a. *Drafting* (writing a rough first version of your paper)

b. Improving your draft by *revising* it (reading and rereading your writing and making changes to improve your organization, development, and vocabulary use)

c. *Editing* your errors (correcting sentence structure, grammar, spelling, and punctuation errors)

You will use your information chart and essay map to begin to draft your essay. You do not need to draft the paragraphs of your essay in the order in which they will appear.

Background Paragraphs

A background paragraph follows an essay's introduction. The purpose of the background paragraph is to prepare readers for the material that is presented in the essay. Deciding what to include in a background paragraph depends largely on:

- The topic
- Your audience
- The purpose of the assignment
- The research you conducted

No matter what the topic is, however, the background paragraph is generally composed of fundamental concepts, terminology, processes, facts, and/or theories that familiarize readers with the topic.

To select material for your background paragraph, return to the information you gathered for your essay. The following strategies may help you select material for your background paragraph:

1. Review the ideas in your essay map.
2. Review the notes you included in your information chart.
3. Review readings that you located, and notice ideas you highlighted and questions you wrote as you began your research.
4. Consider your reader audience. By now, you have read a lot about your topic, so you have developed a knowledge base on this topic. However, your readers may not share this same knowledge. For example, what keywords and terms might your audience need to have defined in order to understand your topic?
5. Ask yourself information questions, like *who? what? when? where? why?* and *how?* Responses to these questions may be included in your paragraph.

EXERCISE **14** **Drafting your background paragraph**

For this essay, you will draft your background paragraph first. Your background paragraph should include factual and/or historical information about the amendment you chose to write about.

1. To help you select important information, review your essay map and information chart, and respond to the following questions:

   - Do you need to give some history about your topic to "set the scene" for your readers? For example: When was this amendment proposed? Who originally proposed and supported it, and why? Was the proposed amendment controversial, or was it agreed upon without much debate?
   - What are some important words and expressions associated with this amendment? Should any of these be defined for your readers?
   - What other information do your readers need to know to understand the rest of the essay?

2. Draft your background paragraph.
3. Include cohesion devices (repetition of keywords/phrases, logical organizers, different forms of a word, and pronouns) to help your readers understand the connection of your ideas.
4. Include in-text citations for all outside sources referred to or included in your paragraph.
5. Add outside source information to your reference page.

SPOTLIGHT ON WRITING SKILLS

Revising and Editing

Revising and editing are important stages in the writing process. When you revise, you reread your writing and make changes to improve your organization, development, and vocabulary use. After revising, spend time editing your writing—that is, correcting your grammar, spelling, and punctuation.

EXERCISE **15** **Revising your background paragraph**

Review and revise your own writing.

1. Read your background paragraph carefully, and consider these questions:

   - Does your paragraph begin with a topic sentence that has a topic and controlling idea(s)?
   - Have you adequately provided factual and/or historical information about your amendment?
   - Should you provide more supporting information to help your readers better understand the amendment?
   - Have you included in-text citations when you used outside sources?
   - Have you used a variety of attribution signals with your paraphrases and quotes?
   - Does your reference page include all outside sources referred to or included in your paragraph?

2. Make any changes needed to improve the meaning of your writing.
3. Save your writing as a word-processed document, and print one copy.

SPOTLIGHT ON WRITING SKILLS

Peer Feedback

You can improve your writing by receiving feedback from other readers, like your classmates. *Peer feedback* is an important part of the writing process because what may seem clear or obvious to you, the writer, is often not so for readers who are newly introduced to the topic. Peer readers can identify areas of your writing that seem unclear, and they can tell you what parts they think are the most interesting.

You do not need to follow all the suggestions offered by your peers, but it is important to keep an open mind and carefully consider your peers' advice.

EXERCISE 16 **Receiving and giving peer feedback**

Receive and give feedback by following these steps:

1. Exchange papers with a partner, and read your partner's paragraph. Do not hold a pen or pencil in your hand during this first reading.

2. Read the paragraph again. This time, on your partner's paper, underline the topic sentence.

3. In the margin of the paper, write the type(s) of supporting information used. For example:

   facts or statistics   expert opinions
   descriptions   explanations
   examples   personal experiences
   observations

4. Tell your partner what you like best about the writing. In the margin, write a statement like:

   Your writing helped me better understand this amendment.

   This historical fact is very interesting.

   I learned some new vocabulary by reading your paragraph.

5. Give one suggestion to improve your partner's writing. In the margin, write a statement like:

   I don't understand the meaning of this sentence.

   I think you should add some more historical information.

   You need to include the source of this information.

6. Ask one question you have about the topic that was not answered in the paragraph. In the margin, write a question like:

   What are the credentials of your expert?

   Why does this amendment cause so much controversy?

   When was this amendment proposed?

7. With your partner, discuss your ideas and suggestions for her or his paragraph.

EXERCISE 17   Editing your background paragraph

Reread your paragraph and consider the suggestions from your peer(s). Make at least two or three changes to improve your writing. Then, edit for grammar, punctuation, and spelling to reflect your best work. Be sure to save your revisions in a word-processed document. You will use this paragraph in your expository paper. Your instructor may also want you to submit your paragraph for review or evaluation.

SPOTLIGHT ON WRITING SKILLS

Body Paragraphs

Body paragraphs are often considered the "meat" of an essay. It is in the body paragraphs that you develop and explain each of the controlling ideas mentioned in your thesis statement. Most academic essays contain between two and six body paragraphs. For each body paragraph in your essay, you should:

- Begin with a topic sentence that expresses the main idea of that paragraph and contains both a main idea and a controlling idea
- Introduce your first major supporting point
- Explain and illustrate that point with specific examples and details
- Use logical organizers to show the relationship between ideas
- Introduce your second major supporting point
- Explain and illustrate that point with specific examples and details
- End with a brief concluding sentence
- Include in-text citations for any sources used

EXERCISE 18   Planning and drafting your body paragraphs

The chapter's writing assignment states that your expository essay should include two or three body paragraphs that explain the meaning of the amendment you chose to research and write about. You should illustrate the guarantees of the amendment by providing supporting information.

1. To help you draft your body paragraphs, review your essay map and information chart.

2. Use the skills you have practiced so far to develop two or three body paragraphs for your essay. In addition to the suggestions about body paragraphs listed previously:

   ■ Include cohesion devices to help your readers understand the connection of your ideas
   ■ Use a variety of attribution signals

3. Add all outside source information to your reference page.

4. Add and save your body paragraphs to your word-processed document. Your instructor may want you to submit your writing for review or evaluation.

SPOTLIGHT ON WRITING SKILLS

Establishing Credibility of Experts

In academic writing, support your explanations and claims with ideas and information from experts on your topic. People can become experts on a topic in various ways, including receiving an academic degree or having extensive experience or observation on the topic. When you cite experts in your paper, provide information about their qualifications or credentials to show your readers why they are trustworthy.

Weak Example:

attribution signal   expert   (year of publ),   paraphrase
According to Hudson (2004), schools are increasingly regulating what students may wear through dress-code and uniform policies, some of which may be unconstitutional.

The reader may not know who Hudson is, so the reader may doubt his credibility.

Stronger Example:

attribution signal   expert   (year of publ)   credentials of expert
According to Hudson (2004), a research attorney for the
                                                    paraphrase
First Amendment Center, schools are increasingly regulating what students may wear through dress-code and uniform policies, some of which may be unconstitutional.

Information about Hudson's credentials is provided. He seems to be a reliable source.

POWER GRAMMAR

Using Non-restrictive Relative Clauses and Appositives to Establish Credibility of Experts

You can provide information about an expert's qualifications or credentials by using *non-restrictive relative clauses* or *appositives*.

1. Paraphrase

Ryan Cooper, who is president of the Young Americans for Freedom, is leading an effort to repeal policies that regulate when, where and how protests, demonstrations and rallies can be held on campuses (Jenson, 2005).

Quotation

According to Benjamin Bull, who is a Phoenix attorney representing a University of Houston student, "The First Amendment is intended to protect unpopular speech because popular speech doesn't have to be protected" (Cody, 2005, p. 18).

A non-restrictive relative clause gives information about a noun. The clause comes immediately after the noun (e.g., your expert) and is surrounded by commas. In the first example, a non-restrictive relative clause provides information about the proper noun, Ryan Cooper. The non-restrictive relative clause explains why Cooper is a credible expert.

The second example also illustrates the use of a non-restrictive relative clause to provide information about Benjamin Bull's credentials.

2. Paraphrase

According to an article in the *Janesville Gazette*, a judge took the unusual step of ordering a newspaper not to publish the testimony that a reporter heard in open court. Mark Atkins, an attorney for the *West Central Tribune*, argued that the order violated the First Amendment (Hardman, 2005).

An appositive (also known as a reduced relative clause) gives information about a noun. An appositive can be called a reduced relative clause because the relative pronoun and verb of the clause are omitted. The appositive comes immediately after the noun (e.g., your expert) and is surrounded by

<u>Quotation</u>
Efforts such as diversity curricula and sensitivity policies have led students and faculty "to fight for the right to express opinions that citizens outside of academia would simply take for granted," declared Sara Lukin, the legal director of the Foundation for Rights in Education (Wald, 2005, p. 23).

commas. In the first example, the expert (Mark Atkins) is followed by an appositive that provides Atkins's credentials.

Likewise, in the second example, Lukin's credibility is illustrated in the appositive.

EXERCISE 19   **Establishing credibility of experts**

Review the paragraphs you have drafted for your essay. Locate instances where you included experts. If you have not yet done so, include information to explain their credibility. Write both non-restrictive relative clauses and appositives.

Examples:

appositive
In her 1995 book, Linda Monk, writer and Harvard Law School graduate, explained that the First Amendment supports tolerance of diversity.

non-restrictive relative clause
Kenneth Starck, who is a professor at the University of Iowa, wrote an article in *Journalism Studies* that encourages U.S. reporters to take greater responsibility for what they report (2004).

Introductory Paragraphs

Readers form impressions about your topic when they read the introductory paragraph of your essay, so it is important to have an interesting, clear opening to your essay. Introductory paragraphs in academic essays have three main functions. An introductory paragraph should:

- Stimulate your readers' interest in your topic
- Provide brief information (approximately one to four sentences) about your topic
- Include a thesis statement that explains the focus of your essay

Introductory paragraphs can begin with:

- A question that you answer in your essay
- A quotation related to your topic
- An interesting brief story
- A fact or statistic that is interesting and relates to your topic
- A definition of an important term or concept discussed in your essay
- A general non-controversial statement about the topic
- A provocative or interesting statement

Master Student Tip

Some writers find it helpful to draft their introductory and concluding paragraphs after they have drafted their background and body paragraphs.

EXERCISE 20   Analyzing introductory paragraphs

Work with a classmate to analyze the following introductory paragraphs and the comments in the margin. Then, complete the activities that follow each paragraph.

The paragraph begins with an interesting quote.

In-text citation includes the page number of the original quote.

"This" is used to link ideas in two sentences.

A logical organizer (however) signals contrast/shift in topic.

The thesis statement includes the main topic and controlling idea(s).

Introductory Paragraph 1: The Complexity of the First Amendment

"If there is any fixed star in our constitutional constellation, it is that no official, high or petty, can prescribe what shall be orthodox in politics, nationalism, religion, or other matters of opinion or force citizens to confess by word or act their faith therein" (Monk, 1995, p. 29). This statement was written by Supreme Court Justice Robert H. Jackson over 70 years ago. These strong words describe the First Amendment. Most citizens are aware that the First Amendment guarantees fundamental rights like freedom of speech, religion, and the press; however, "freedom" does not carry the same meaning for all people. It is important to study the First Amendment to understand how the interpretation of this document has been applied in different times and situations. This essay examines several recent Supreme Court cases that reveal how complex it is to apply the First Amendment to real life situations.

Reference

Monk, L. (1995). *The First Amendment: America's blueprint for tolerance.* Washington, D.C.: Close Up Foundation Publishing.

In Introductory Paragraph 1,

a. This writer began the introductory paragraph with a quote. What other strategies could the writer have used?

_____

_____

b. Draw arrows to connect the comments in the margin to the features in the paragraph.

c. Draw a box around the main topic in the thesis statement.

d. Circle the controlling idea(s) in the thesis statement.

e. Write three questions you expect to be answered in this essay.

_____

_____

_____

Introductory Paragraph 2: The Nineteenth Amendment

A brief story is presented to engage readers' interest.

To integrate the direct quote into the paragraph, a word is added in brackets [ ].

The website name is cited since no author is given.

The paragraph ends with a thesis statement that explains the topic and controlling ideas of the paper.

On the reference page, a Web address can be divided at any slash (/), period (.), or underscore (_). A final period does not come after the Web address.

The author was not identified for this source, so it is alphabetized by the organization.

The time was before the Civil War, before electricity or the automobile, and before women had rights. Lucy Stone was a young woman who defied her father's and society's views that women should be dominated by men. She educated herself, worked to pay tuition, and enrolled in college. Oberlin College in Massachusetts, where Ms. Stone graduated in 1847, proudly states on its website that "at the low wages then paid to women, it took Lucy nine years to save up enough money to enter college . . . [and] there was only one college that admitted women" (Electronic Oberlin Group, 2003). In fact, Stone became the first woman from Massachusetts to graduate from college. More importantly, she was the first woman to refuse to pay property taxes because she could not vote (Lewis, 2003, para. 22). She and others influenced by her, like Susan B. Anthony, struggled courageously for women's suffrage (the right to vote). This paper describes their fight and discusses its result: the Nineteenth Amendment to the U.S. Constitution, which granted women the right to vote in 1920.

References

Lewis, J.J., (2003). *A soul as free as the air: Profile of Lucy Stone.* Retrieved May 12, 2004, from http://womenshistory.about.com/library/weekly/aa062899.htm

Electronic Oberlin Group. (2003). *Lucy Stone (1818–1893).* Retrieved May 12, 2004, from http://www.oberlin.edu/external/EOG/OYTT-images/LucyStone.html

In Introductory Paragraph 2,

    a. How did the writer begin this introductory paragraph (e.g., with a question, with a fact)? _____

    b. Explain the use of [*and*] that appears in the quotation.

    c. Explain the use of the ellipses mark (. . .).

    d. In the references provided at the end of the paragraph, label the website name, the year it was updated, and the paragraph in which the writer found the information about Ms. Stone's college. Draw a line to connect this information to the in-text citation provided in the paragraph.

    e. Write three questions you expect to be answered in this essay.

_____

_____

_____

_____

_____

_____

EXERCISE 21 **Drafting your introductory paragraph**

Draft your introductory paragraph by following these steps:

    1. Look again at your essay map and the writing you already drafted for this essay.

    2. Carefully consider your "working" thesis statement. Revise it if necessary.

    3. Draft an introductory paragraph that:

        a. Stimulates your readers' interest in the amendment you chose

        b. Provides brief background information

        c. Presents your thesis statement

    4. If you used outside sources, include in-text citations and add source information to your reference page.

    5. Add and save your introductory paragraph to your word-processed document.

SPOTLIGHT ON WRITING SKILLS

Concluding Paragraphs

Just like your introductory paragraph, your concluding paragraph has different purposes:

a. It reminds your readers about the main points developed in your essay by summarizing those ideas.
b. It provides final comments about your topic.

Readers expect to see the main points that were made in the essay repeated in the conclusion. The conclusion is shorter than your body paragraphs because you do not use supporting details. Instead, you should write overall comments about your topic. However, do not surprise readers by taking a new direction or introducing a new idea in your conclusion.

One way to write a successful concluding paragraph is to make a clear reference to a specific idea from the introduction. Mentioning an example or detail from the start of your essay gives your paper a sense of wholeness and finality. For example:

- If you started with a quotation, return to that quote or add another relevant one by the same person in your conclusion
- If you started with a brief story, you might relate how the story ends
- If you used numbers or statistics in your introduction, you can mention those in your conclusion as well
- If you developed your introduction in a chronological manner, you might end with a prediction for the future
- If you began with an interesting statement or comment, you might state the action you want the readers to take
- If you focused on a problem, you can suggest a solution to that problem

EXERCISE 22 Analyzing paragraphs

Analyze the following introductory and concluding paragraphs from the same essay. Draw lines to connect the comments to the appropriate sections in the paragraphs. Then, complete the activities that follow.

The paragraph begins with a general statement and a specific example.

Brief background information is provided.

The paragraph ends with a thesis statement (with the topic and controlling ideas to be developed).

Introductory Paragraph: The Unusual Twenty-first Amendment

Government enacts and enforces rules, or laws, for people to live together in a society. In the United States, for example, government exists on local, state, and national levels, as required by the U.S. Constitution. The Constitution outlines the laws of society in its 27 amendments. Only one amendment, the Twenty-first Amendment, was passed to repeal an earlier amendment. The Twenty-first Amendment ended the prohibition of alcohol in the United States, a law that had been in place due to the Eighteenth Amendment (Janda, Berry, & Goldman, 2002). The relatively quick passage of the Twenty-first Amendment is not surprising when one considers the social climate, the economic situation, and the federal government in the early 1930s.

The paragraph begins with a general statement connected to the introduction.

Readers are reminded of the main ideas.

A prediction is offered.

Concluding Paragraph: The Unusual Twenty-first Amendment

Laws are designed to allow people to live together in a society. Sometimes, however, laws need to change as society changes. The social climate of the 1930s, along with the economic and federal government situations, basically guaranteed the repeal of the Eighteenth Amendment of the U.S. Constitution. Perhaps in the future, our country will see other changes in the Constitutional amendments that reflect the ever-changing culture of our society.

Reference

Janda, K., Berry, J., & Goldman, J. (2002). *The challenge of democracy* (7th ed.). Boston: Houghton Mifflin.

1. How did the writer begin this introductory paragraph (e.g., with a question, with a fact)? _____

2. How did the writer connect the conclusion to the introductory paragraph? _____

   _____

3. Underline the topic and circle the controlling idea(s) in the thesis statement. _____

   _____

4. Circle the controlling ideas mentioned in the conclusion.
5. What main points do you think were addressed in this essay?

   _____

   _____

   _____

   _____

EXERCISE 23 Drafting your concluding paragraph

Plan and draft your concluding paragraph by completing these steps:

1. Read through your entire essay one more time to prepare to write the conclusion.
2. Identify a way to refer to the introduction in your concluding paragraph.
3. Identify and summarize one or two main ideas from the body paragraphs that you will refer to in the conclusion. Use these ideas to refresh the readers' memory of the main points.
4. Decide what final comments you can offer on the topic, but do not introduce new information.
5. Decide what strategy you will use to end your concluding paragraph (e.g., add a prediction, recommendation, solution).
6. Draft your concluding paragraph.
7. Add and save the conclusion to your word-processed document.

EXERCISE 24   Revising your expository essay

Reread your entire essay from the introductory paragraph to the concluding paragraph.

1. To make sure that you adequately fulfilled the requirements of the assignment, review the details of the chapter's writing assignment.
2. Then, slowly and thoughtfully reread your entire essay. Make revisions where appropriate.
3. Review your reference page to be sure that all sources you used when writing your paper are included. Use the format of the reference page in Appendix 3, "End-of-Text References."
4. Print a copy of your expository essay.

EXERCISE 25   Providing and receiving peer feedback

Work with a partner, and exchange copies of your expository essay.

1. Review your partner's essay, without commenting, to become familiar with the topic.
2. To offer feedback to your partner, use a peer review sheet located at the website for this book: http://esl.college.hmco.com/students.
3. Return and discuss your partner's essay.

EXERCISE 26   Finalizing your essay

Finalize your essay by completing the following:

1. Consider your partner's suggestions and your own insights as you revise your essay.
2. Edit for and correct any errors in grammar, spelling, and punctuation.
3. Save the document as your final draft, and print one copy.
4. Attach your draft(s) and copies of all outside sources referred to while you wrote your paper.
5. Submit your paper and attachments for your instructor's review and evaluation.

☐ More Practice and Self-Assessment

1. Return to the chapter objectives on the first page of the chapter. Read each objective, and put a check mark in the appropriate box: "I have learned this well" or "I need to work on this." Be honest. You will continue to work on similar writing skills throughout this course, and diagnosing current weaknesses helps you focus on improving those areas. Share your objectives chart with your instructor.

2. Make a list of at least five conventions of expository writing.

3. Watch the TV news or read a current newspaper article that reports on a lawsuit that involves a violation of one of the amendments. Write a paragraph explaining who is involved in the lawsuit and why.

4. Write an expository paragraph of about two hundred fifty words in response to one of these questions:

   a. What one area of life is most notably affected by Amendment *x*? (Fill in "*x*" with the amendment you focused on in your expository essay.)

   b. Why is it beneficial to study the U.S. Constitution and its amendments?

   c. What necessary steps must academic writers follow to produce an effective expository essay?

   d. What have you learned about yourself as a writer of academic English in this chapter?

WEB POWER

For additional exercises related to the content in this chapter, go to **http://esl.college.hmco.com/students**.

Writing an Analytical Report

Many academic assignments require you to write a report in which you analyze a topic. To analyze a topic:

- **Look at the causes, reasons, or factors that contribute to an end result**
- **Describe, present, or explain this information**

When you write analytical reports, you use expository writing skills—that is, you explain ideas and events and illustrate those explanations by providing facts, examples, and descriptions. Examples of academic analytical reports are laboratory reports, book reports, and article summaries.

Chapter Objectives

Read the following chapter objectives to preview the chapter content. After you complete the chapter, return to this chart and check (✓) the appropriate boxes on the right.	I have learned this well.	I need to work on this.
Follow a 3-step writing process to gather, oganize, and draft information		
Identify and select credible websites		
Develop library research skills		
Practice active reading strategies		
Construct an information chart to synthesize information		
Understand essay development for analytical reports		
Create an essay map to organize information		
Understand acronym use in academic writing		
Identify definition structures in academic writing		
Include definitions of key terms in your essay		
Use paraphrasing techniques		
Cite sources within your essay		
Draft an end-of-text reference list		

Chapter Writing Assignment

You will research an epidemic—a disease that has affected a large portion of a given population either in historical or present times—to explain this epidemic and illustrate its significance in a three- or four-page analytical report. This assignment requires you to complete Internet and library searches and to learn some biological terms and concepts, especially those related to viruses and immunology. You will analyze, organize, and synthesize information gathered from a variety of sources. Your report must include the following:

- An introductory paragraph
- A background paragraph that includes factual and/or historical information about the epidemic you choose
- Two or three body paragraphs that explain the epidemic and illustrate its significance
- A concluding paragraph
- At least two to four in-text citations
- An end-of-text reference page with references for all sources referred to as you wrote your report

To complete your analytical report for this chapter, you will follow the three-step writing process that is used throughout this text:

1. Gathering Information
2. Focusing and Organizing
3. Drafting, Revising, and Editing

☐ Gathering Information

 EXERCISE 1 Discussing and writing about disease

Gather information about epidemics by completing these steps:

1. With your instructor and classmates, select and discuss two or three diseases you have heard about. Here are some to consider:

AIDS	polio	dengue fever	mad cow disease
malaria	leptospirosis	yellow fever	Ebola virus
bird flu	SARS	bubonic plague	tuberculosis
anthrax	influenza	West Nile virus	monkeypox

2. In your discussion, try to answer some of these questions and take notes on points being discussed.
   ▪ Where did the disease originate?
   ▪ What are the symptoms of the disease?
   ▪ What do you know about the cause(s) of the disease?
   ▪ What effect(s) does the disease have on individuals and society?
   ▪ What treatments, if any, exist?

3. Write for five minutes to explain what you learned or know about one of these diseases. Use some of the ideas discussed with your class.

4. Place your writing in your notebook or folder for future reference.

SPOTLIGHT ON WRITING SKILLS

Active Reading Strategies

To write about a disease—or any other topic you are assigned in college—you must read about the topic from a variety of sources. Active reading means practicing strategies that help you understand concepts. Active readers "mark up" their materials as they read. They underline, highlight, and write questions and notes in the margins. In particular, they:

■ Focus on the main idea and controlling idea(s) in a reading passage
■ Identify facts, statistics, explanations, and examples that support the main ideas
■ Note keywords, topic-specific terminology, and definitions provided in the reading
■ Note names of important people or groups involved in the topic
■ Identify interesting or important historical background information
■ Look for similarities and differences in various sources about the same topic

EXERCISE 2 Practicing active reading strategies

Read the following paragraphs, and use active reading strategies to identify, mark, and note important points, details, and terms. The first paragraph has been started for you.

Paragraph 1: Black Death

topic = Black Death ⟶

controlling idea =
economic crisis ⟶

started in 1331
by fleas/rats ⟶

    In the fourteenth century, Europe was struggling with an economic crisis. The Black Death, or the bubonic plague, added to this crisis. <u>This disease was carried by fleas</u> on rats and probably first <u>struck Mongolia in 1331–1332</u>. From there, it crossed into Russia. Carried back from Black Sea ports, the plague <u>reached Sicily in 1347</u>. Spreading swiftly throughout much of Europe, it attacked an already declining and undernourished population. The first onslaught lasted until 1351, and other serious outbreaks occurred in later decades. The crowded cities and towns had the highest mortalities. Perhaps twenty million people—about one-quarter to one-third of the European population—perished in the worst natural disaster in recorded history.

Source: Perry, M., Baker, J.W., & Hollinger, P. (2003). *The humanities in the western tradition*. Boston: Houghton Mifflin.

Paragraph 2: Spread of AIDS

    The AIDS epidemic in Africa is unlikely to remain confined to Africa. The country's strains of HIV, if left unchecked, are sure to spread elsewhere and overwhelm whatever resources we have devoted to defeating our Western-based strains. Other highly populous countries, like China and India, are just beginning to feel the brunt of the disease. There is a perversely poetic loopiness at work: a disease that presumably had its origins in Africa made its first angry mark in America, then exploded in Africa, and is now moving onward, outward, and back again. It is not Africa's health crisis alone.

Source: Angier, N. (2003). Together, in sickness and in health. *Global politics in a changing world*. Boston: Houghton Mifflin.

Paragraph 3: Yellow Fever

Recent years have seen an increasing, rather than decreasing, incidence of viral diseases that had, supposedly, been under control. Chief among these is yellow fever—an epidemic that spread throughout Florida at the end of the 19th century and killed thousands of people. Yellow fever is still endemic throughout the tropics, despite there having been extensive eradication and vaccination campaigns over several decades. Now it is threatening to again spread to more temperate zones, including the continental U.S., largely as a result of inadvertent importation of vector mosquitoes transported from Asia to the United States.

Source: Rybicki, R. (2002). *Emerging and re-emerging viral diseases: A challenge for biotechnology.* Retrieved July 16, 2003, from http://www.micro.msb.le.ac.uk/335/Emerging2.html

---

EXERCISE 3 **Analyzing a student report**

Use active reading skills to understand the following student report. Then, with a partner, complete the activities that follow.

Student Analytical Report

Opening comments attempt to capture the readers' interest.

An attribution signal explains the credibility of statistics.

The thesis statement indicates three controlling ideas.

Many people living in Asia are wearing filter masks in public places. This is not a fashion statement. The masks are due to SARS. Severe acute respiratory syndrome, commonly referred to as SARS, is a respiratory illness that has recently been reported in Asia, North America, South America, and Europe. According to a report by the Centers for Disease Control and Prevention (CDC), close to 9,000 people have become sick with SARS and nearly 1,000 have died across the world (CDC, 2004). Since this disease is spread by close person-to-person contact, the infection percentage is quite high. For this reason, people should understand how SARS is spread, how to treat it, and how it affects societies.

Historical information is provided in the background paragraph.

Credible agencies are mentioned.

A pronoun (*they*) refers to previously mentioned organizations and builds coherence.

A topic sentence introduces the controlling idea (how SARS is spread).

A quote is introduced with an attribution signal.

A logical organizer (*however*) connects sentences & illustrates opposing ideas. See Appendix 4 for more information.

The focus of the second body paragraph is on the controlling idea (treatment).

The definition of a term (*antibiotics*) is provided in parentheses ( ). The source does not include a date, so the citation states "n.d." (no date).

SARS was first recognized as a major health threat in early 2003. Within a few months, the disease spread to other countries. The World Health Organization (WHO) and the CDC worked closely with federal groups and health departments in an effort to stop the spread of the virus (CDC, 2004). They also worked hard to educate the public about the symptoms of the disease. The CDC (2003) reports that the main symptoms of SARS include headache, muscle soreness, high fever (100.4 degree Fahrenheit or more), and coughing. Most sufferers of SARS also develop pneumonia. When these symptoms are severe, the result can be death.

SARS is a contagious disease that spreads very fast. In fact, according to a *New York Times* article, "249 individual cases of SARS could all be traced to one man. . . . Of those infected, 214 were medical personnel or health-care workers" (Neer, n.d., p. 16). Close contact with an infected person is needed for the virus to spread from one person to another. Aerosolized droplets that are exhaled when a patient breathes and bodily secretions from an infected person both spread the disease (CDC, 2004). However, the amount of the virus needed to cause an infection in others has not yet been determined. To date, the majority of cases have occurred in hospital workers who have cared for SARS patients and the close family members of these patients.

While some medicines have been tried, at this time, there are no drugs available to treat SARS. In fact, there is little that doctors can do to treat this disease. Antibiotics (drugs designed to treat bacterial infections) do not appear to be effective. Instead, the best that can currently be done is to take precautionary measures and, once the virus has been contracted, to treat the symptoms. Some precautionary measures for medical personnel include washing hands regularly, wearing and frequently discarding disposable gowns and gloves, and wearing eye protection (Neer, n.d.). It is very important that patients suspected of having SARS be seen by protected health professionals who should isolate the patient.

A topic sentence
introduces the
controlling idea
(effects of SARS).

A quote from an
expert is provided
as supporting
information. The
expert's credentials
are indicated.

Main points are
reviewed in the
conclusion.

Final comments are
offered (a
recommendation).

In addition to deaths, SARS has had negative effects on the public economy. In 2003, WHO recommended that people not travel to certain areas of the world—like Hong Kong, mainland China, and Taiwan—which experienced higher rates of SARS (Online NewsHour, 2003). These warnings shocked national economies since many people were afraid to travel to certain areas of the world due to fear of exposure to SARS. For instance, numerous travelers and businesspeople canceled their trips to Asia. These cancellations had a negative impact on the Asian tourism industry. Dr. Su Ih-jen, Taiwan's director of disease control, was quoted as saying, "If the travel advisory was not removed, Taiwan's economy could not stand much longer" (Online NewsHour, 2003, para. 3).

Indeed, SARS is a serious disease that has caused human death and destruction to several countries' tourism economies. This illness has spread globally in a short period of time. However, SARS does not have to be highly contagious. Protective measures, such as washing hands, can decrease the chance of spreading the disease. Until treatments can be identified, prevention is the most important thing. The global community must work together to prevent SARS from doing further damage.

Outside sources referred to or included in this report are listed on a separate page at the end of the report.

For many of these sources, the author was not identified, so the source is alphabetized by the organization.

When the publishing date is not provided, include the abbreviation "n.d." for "no date."

References

Centers for Disease Control and Prevention. (2004, January 13). *Fact sheet: Basic information about SARS*. Retrieved April 1, 2004, from http://www.cdc.giv/ncidod/sars/factsheet.htm

Centers for Disease Control and Prevention. (2003, January 28). *Frequently asked questions about SARS*. Retrieved April 1, 2004, from http://www.cdc.gov/ncidod/sars/faq.htm

Neer, K. (n.d.). *How SARS works*. Retrieved April 1, 2004, from http://science.howstuffworks.com/sars.htm

Online NewsHour. (2003, June). *The emergence of SARS*. Retrieved April 1, 2004, from http://www.pbs.org/newshour/health/sars/

1. Circle and connect the controlling ideas in the thesis statement with similar controlling ideas in the topic sentences.

2. In the margins of each body paragraph, identify three or four uses of supporting information. Examples:

facts or statistics	expert opinions	descriptions
explanations	examples	personal experiences
observations		

3. In each body paragraph, circle and connect uses of cohesion devices that help the reader understand the connection of ideas. In addition to the connection of controlling ideas in the thesis and topic sentences that you identified in #1, coherence may include:

   - Repetition of key words and phrases
   - Logical organizers
   - Different forms of a word

4. Draw a box around uses of in-text citation. How many paraphrases are included in this report? _____ How many quotations are included? _____

5. Underline examples of attribution signals. How many attribution signals are included in this report? _____

6. Identify places where the writer has shown credibility of experts. Place an asterisk (*) next to examples.

SPOTLIGHT ON WRITING SKILLS

Credible Websites

Many of the sources you collect for your report will come from the Internet or library databases. It is important to check that the sources you include and cite in your paper are credible. *A credible source* consistently reports information in an accurate and complete manner.

One clue to the credibility of a source is the "expertise" of the author, which you can identify by looking for information about the author's training, education, or experience. First, look at the *homepage* of the site. To find the homepage, delete the words in the website address (the URL) after the *domain name* (e.g., .edu, .com). For example, in the URL *http://www.cdc.gov/ncidod/dvbid/plague/index.htm*, you would keep only *http://www.cdc.gov* to find the homepage. You can also type an author's name into an online *search engine* (a program, such as Google or Yahoo, that finds specific information across the World Wide Web). Then, open a few of the items displayed. In this way, you can learn about the writer's professional background, research, and/or publications.

Another clue to the credibility of a website is its domain, or source. This information can be found in the URL even before you access the site. Look for websites maintained by educational institutions (.edu), governmental agencies (.gov), and nonprofit organizations (.org). These domains signal different purposes for websites, but each is usually considered a credible domain. Many other organizations maintain informative websites, but the content on the site may try to persuade readers about a special interest. The same is true for commercial sites (.com), which may try to persuade readers about a product.

The following list of websites was compiled by a student conducting research for a report on the bubonic plague. The domain names consist of the three letters that are circled in each URL.

URL (website address)	Domain (source)
http://www.bocklabs.wisc.edu/ed.html	edu = education site
http://www.cdc.gov/ncidod/dvbid/plague/index.html	gov = government site
http://www.pbs.org/wgbh/amex/influenza	org = organization site
http://search.epnet.com/direct.asp?an=3333990&db=aph	com = commercial site

Following is a list of questions you can ask about any website to help you assess its credibility.

Is This Web Source Credible?	
Questions	**Comments**
1. Is the domain trustworthy/credible?	If the domain is .gov, .edu, or .org, it probably is credible. Other sites can be credible, too, but you need to assess them carefully.
2. Is information about the author (e.g., the name) given?	If author information is not included, assess the credibility of the agency or organization.

Is This Web Source Credible?	
Questions	**Comments**
3. Are the author's credentials listed (or a link provided)?	Often the titles *professor*, *research associate*, and *doctor* indicate credibility.
4. Does the author and/or site have a credible affiliation?	If yes, then the author is likely to be credible.
5. Is a date of publication or revision given?	The date can give you clues about accuracy and timeliness of the information provided.
6. Are references listed at the end?	Look at the sources to see if they are credible. If so, this site may be credible, too.
7. Are links to other good sources of information given?	Again, if so, this site may be credible, too.
8. Is the information objective (i.e., contains no persuasive language)?	Persuasive language often means the site wants you to agree with a certain viewpoint. Be careful; such sites may not present both sides of an issue.
9. Is the page void of any advertising?	Advertisements may mean the site wants you to agree with a viewpoint. Be careful.
10. Is this a credible source for an academic paper?	If the majority of your responses are yes, this site is most likely credible.

WEB POWER

The questions listed in the "Spotlight on Writing Skills" box are basic questions to ask about any source of information (paper or online). In addition, there are some great online resources to help you evaluate websites as credible sources for use in an academic paper. Visit the website for this book at http://esl.college.hmco.com/students.

EXERCISE 4 Selecting your topic by searching the Internet

For this chapter's writing assignment, select one illness that has affected a large portion of a given population, either in historical or present times. In Exercise 1, you discussed various diseases and wrote about one. However, your knowledge about that disease may be limited. For this exercise, make a final decision about your topic for this chapter.

1. Begin by searching some informative, credible websites maintained by government agencies and health organizations. Browse through several to familiarize yourself with past and current epidemics. Select one that interests you. Following are a few homepages whose sites contain search engines and links to credible information on diseases.

Centers for Disease Control and Prevention	http://www.cdc.gov
U.S. Department of Health and Human Services	http://www.os.dhhs.gov
U.S. Food and Drug Administration	http://www.fda.gov
National Institutes of Health	http://www.nih.gov
National Institute of Allergy and Infectious Diseases	http://www.niaid.nih.gov
World Health Organization	http://www.who.int
United Nations Children's Fund	http://www.unicef.org

   Other useful sites are SciCentral.com, USNews.com, Accessexcellence.org, and Medlineplus.gov.

2. As you browse articles online, note the use of different names used to describe the same illness. The bubonic plague, for instance, is often referred to as "The Black Death" or simply "the plague." Influenza may be called "the flu." If possible, write at least two names you can use for the disease you chose:

3. If you find alternatives to the infectious disease you are researching, try typing these different names into a search engine, like Google or Yahoo, to find more results. Locate and print at least **four** credible sources of information on the disease you chose to study. Remember to print the homepage of the website in order to cite the reference properly, or record this information on your documents.

Master Student Tip

When you look for books on a disease—or any other topic—notice other books nearby. Books about the same subjects are shelved in one area. Look above and below and to the left and right of the book you are trying to locate for other books that look interesting and helpful.

SPOTLIGHT ON WRITING SKILLS

Library Resources

You may be accustomed to the convenience and relative effectiveness of conducting searches online, but when gathering information for an academic paper, do not limit yourself to the Internet. After you have chosen your topic and have completed a preliminary Internet search, your next step is to visit your campus library. Libraries house many materials that you cannot access on the Web. Equally important, trained librarians can assist you in gathering information on your topic. Ask a librarian to help you locate some of the following types of sources on the disease you chose to study:

1. Print materials such as:

    - Books you may borrow from the library
    - Reference materials you can use only in the library (and make copies of select pages)
      Example: *Encyclopedia Library of Health and Living*
    - Current and past issues of professional journals, magazines, and popular academic magazines
      Examples: *New England Journal of Medicine; U.S. News & World Report*
    - Materials that are placed on reserve by college instructors
      Examples: textbooks, journal articles, research reports, lecture notes

2. Multimedia materials such as:

    - Videos, CDs, and DVDs
      Examples: documentaries, media supplements to textbooks

EXERCISE 5 Gathering information from the library

*Visit your college library. If you can, go with a classmate who is also working on this assignment. Find at least **three** credible sources of information during this visit. If you have questions about using the library or about locating credible sources, ask a librarian. Librarians are there to help you.*

1. Search for books you can borrow from the library.
   a. Write down the call numbers of at least two books, and then locate them in the stacks (the shelves of books in the library).
   b. Look for a *table of contents* in the beginning and/or an *index* at the end of any factual book. Read through the lists of subjects covered and decide if this book would be helpful for your report.
2. Search for informative reference books you can use in the library.
   a. Find the reference area in the library, and look for books on medicine, health, and disease.
   b. Browse several reference books for information on your disease.
   c. Photocopy pages of the book(s) that contain information you can use for your report. Also photocopy (or write down) the title of the book, the author(s) or editor(s), the publisher, the place and date of publication, and the page numbers copied. You will need all this information to cite references in your report.
   d. Do not tear out a page from or mark on the original document—just mark your copies.
3. Search for articles in publications that the library subscribes to online.
   a. Ask a librarian for the password to access online databases to which the library subscribes.
   b. Type the name of your disease topic into the search engine of several different databases. Two common ones are EBSCO and JSTOR. Browse research publications, news articles from magazines and newspapers, and other academic publications. Select the most understandable and informative articles about your topic to print for closer reading later.
4. Make sure you gather all the materials you printed, copied, or borrowed from the library before you leave. Do not attempt to return materials to their shelves. Sometimes materials can get misplaced this way. Instead, leave them on the table for library personnel to re-shelve.

> **Master Student Tip**
>
> Many online databases contain an e-mail function. You can e-mail an article to yourself and save on printing costs at the library. Be sure the full citation is included (for your reference page in your report).

**Master
Student Tip**

Remember your reader audience. As you gather and select information about your topic, note what terminology is difficult to understand and what material initially puzzles or surprises you. Pay attention to examples and explanations that help answer questions you have about the subject. You should include these definitions, examples, and explanations in your report to help readers better understand your topic.

EXERCISE 6   Using active reading strategies

Review the materials you gathered during your online and library searches. You should have about four online and three library sources.

Select at least three of those sources, and read them carefully, using active reading strategies. That is, underline, highlight, and write notes and questions in the margins.

SPOTLIGHT ON WRITING SKILLS

Acronyms in Academic Writing

When discussing diseases, acronyms are often used. *Acronyms* are short words made up of the first letters of several words or their parts to form one name. Examples are AIDS (acquired immune deficiency syndrome), DNA (deoxyribonucleic acid), and HHS (U.S. Department of Health and Human Services).

In academic writing, the convention is to use the full name of a term or organization the first time it appears in a report or article, followed by its common acronym in parentheses. Then, when it is mentioned again, the acronym is used by itself.

Example

The National Institutes of Health (NIH) recently awarded $24 million to Chiron Corporation to test a vaccine. NIH hopes to publish preliminary results of the Chiron study in ten to twelve months.

EXERCISE 7   Identifying acronyms

With a small group of classmates, write out the names of the following acronyms. If you do not know the meaning of an acronym, check a dictionary or ask another group. Many dictionaries include common acronyms in their listings. You will become more familiar with these acronyms as you work through this chapter.

Example

NIAID   *National Institute of Allergy and Infectious Diseases*

1. SARS   _____

2. CDC   _____

3. TB   _____

4. WHO   _____

5. HIV   _____

6. FDA   _____

7. HHS   _____

8. AMA   _____

9. UNESCO   _____

10. USAID   _____

☐ Focusing and Organizing

SPOTLIGHT ON WRITING SKILLS

Information Charts to Synthesize Ideas

Recall from Chapter 1 that an information chart is a multicolumn chart that helps you visualize and organize main ideas and supporting information. An information chart helps you synthesize information; that is, it helps you develop your report by including supporting information from a variety of sources. The following is one possible format for an information chart for this chapter's report. This chart includes information from one source; however, your own chart should include additional sources.

Information Chart for a Report on Tuberculosis

Source, date, author, and credentials (for citation purposes)	Facts and/ or historical information	Symptoms	Causes/ effects	Other factors
American Lung Assoc, April 2004, www.lungusa. Treatment— org/diseases/ lungtb/html	Infectious disease, attacks lungs 10 million Americans infected; 10% will develop TB (para. 2) 2 million deaths each year	Persistent cough, fatigue, weight loss, loss of appetite, fever, coughing blood, night sweats (para. 3)	Not easy to be infected. Must come in close contact (family, close friends) (para. 5)	TB skin test—find out if infected (para. 4) preventive therapy (daily dose of isoniazid, up to 6+ months) (para. 4)

Master Student Tip

If the website does not contain a date of publication or revision (e.g., Last Revised January 2005), then record the date that you retrieved the information. You will need to cite this date if you decide to refer to this information in your report.

EXERCISE 8 **Constructing an information chart**

You already have knowledge about your chosen topic, but an information chart is helpful for synthesizing sources.

1. To help you synthesize ideas from a variety of sources, create a five-column information chart like the previous example.
2. Review the notes and questions you included on the readings you located, and fill in the chart. Specifically:

   ▪ When completing the "Source/Author" column, include information that helps you establish the author's credentials.

- In all the columns, write keywords and phrases that remind you about the ideas.
- Include only a few direct quotations because it is best to paraphrase others' ideas.
- Include page or paragraph numbers of original sources so that you can return to them if you need additional information when you draft your report.

3. Review the information you included in your chart, and highlight significant pieces of information you want to include in your report.

EXERCISE 9 Discussing and sharing information

Exchange information about your topic by following these steps:

1. With two or three classmates who (if possible) are writing about the same disease, discuss your topic. Share your information chart and your outside sources.

   - Take turns discussing specific information you located, like interesting historical information about the disease or facts and statistics.
   - Share useful readings you discovered, and explain why the readings are particularly useful.

2. Take notes about information your classmates located that you might also consider using in your report. For example, you might record:

   - Interesting facts and statistics
   - Important dates
   - Key terms and their definitions
   - Key people involved in the research of the disease and their findings
   - Useful quotes from experts

3. Be sure to record citation information for any details you might include in your report and/or any documents you might refer to when drafting your report.

4. Save your chart in a notebook or folder. Your instructor may also want to collect a copy of your chart for review or evaluation.

SPOTLIGHT ON WRITING SKILLS

Essay Development for Analytical Reports

In an analytical report, you must carefully examine something—like a disease—to fully understand it. Writers often analyze the causes, reasons, effects, and factors related to what they are writing about. For an analytical report about a disease, you might ask:

- ▪ What are the causes of this disease?
- ▪ What factors have contributed to the increased occurrence of this disease?
- ▪ How can the spread of this disease be reduced or eliminated?
- ▪ What are the symptoms of this disease?
- ▪ Why is this disease significant?
- ▪ What might happen because of this disease?

EXERCISE 10 Evaluating thesis statements

Read the following thesis statements from two student reports. For each thesis statement, underline the topic and circle the controlling ideas. Then, for each controlling idea, list one or two questions you expect to be analyzed and answered in the body paragraphs. An example is provided.

Example Thesis Statement

People should understand how <u>SARS</u> is (spread), how to (treat) it, and how it (affects) societies.

Example Questions to be Analyzed and Answered in the Report

1. In what ways is SARS spread?
2. Can SARS be treated or cured? If so, how?
3. How does SARS affect the people who get sick?

Thesis Statement 1

Understanding the causes, symptoms, and treatment of AIDS is essential for people across the world.

Questions to be Analyzed and Answered in the Report

1. —————————————————————————————————

2. —————————————————————————————————

3. —————————————————————————————————

4. —————————————————————————————————

Thesis Statement 2

Yellow fever caused the deaths of thousands of people; however, it had several positive effects, such as the progress of science and the establishment of the State Board of Health in Florida.

Questions to be Analyzed and Answered in the Report

1. —————————————————————————————————

2. —————————————————————————————————

3. —————————————————————————————————

4. —————————————————————————————————

Thesis Statement 3

To prevent the further spread of AIDS, it is important to understand the issues surrounding this disease, including its causes, prevention strategies, and consequences.

Questions to be Analyzed and Answered in the Report

1. —————————————————————————————————

2. —————————————————————————————————

3. —————————————————————————————————

4. —————————————————————————————————

EXERCISE **11** Drafting a thesis statement

Draft a thesis statement for your essay by completing these steps:

1. Review the chapter writing assignment on page 48 and your information chart.
2. Draft a "working" thesis statement for your report that addresses the assignment. Remember, this is a working thesis, and you may modify your thesis as you draft your report.
3. Underline the topic, and circle the controlling ideas in your thesis.
4. Write three to five questions related to your controlling ideas that you plan to answer in the body paragraphs.
5. Save your thesis statement and questions in your notebook or folder or as a word-processed document. Your instructor may also want to collect this information for review or evaluation.

EXERCISE **12** Reviewing and creating an essay map

In Chapter 1, you created an essay map: an outline of the ideas you planned to include in each section of your essay. To create an essay map for this chapter, complete the following:

1. Examine this student essay map created for the report on page 51.

Essay Map: Report on SARS

Introductory Paragraph	*Attract attention: people wearing masks* *Brief info: definition of SARS, statistics*
Thesis Statement	*People should know how contagious SARS is, how to treat it, and how it affects societies*
Background Paragraph *Topic sentence*	*SARS was first recognized as a threat in 2003.*
Support	■ *Brief historical info* ■ *Info on causes* ■ *Symptoms*

Body Paragraph 1 Topic Sentence	SARS is a (contagious) disease that spreads quickly.
Questions to be analyzed:	How many people have been affected? How is SARS spread?
Body Paragraph 2 Topic Sentence	Currently, no drugs to (treat) SARS are available.
Questions to be analyzed:	What can be done to prevent the spread of SARS? What can be done after people have the virus?
Body Paragraph 3 Topic Sentence	SARS has had (negative effects) on the economy.
Questions to be analyzed:	What are the negative effects? What can be done?
Concluding Paragraph	Remind readers of main points Relate to remarks in introduction Provide final comments

2. Construct a working essay map for your report.
   a. Review the readings you gathered, your information chart, your thesis statement, and your questions related to your controlling ideas (from the previous exercise) for ideas and support for your report.
   b. Consider your audience and purpose when constructing your essay map. Write for an audience of the general public, like your classmates. Consider what your readers know and do not know about your topic. Your purpose is to educate your readers about your chosen disease.
   c. Create an essay map by listing the components of the report on the left side of a sheet of paper. On the right side, include your plans to develop your report. Remember, this is a working essay map, and you may revise it as you develop your report.

SPOTLIGHT ON WRITING SKILLS

Introductory and Background Paragraphs

The introductory paragraph of an academic essay provides brief information (one to four sentences) about the essay's topic. Often, this information includes key terms and their definitions to help readers understand the essay. In addition, most academic writing assignments benefit from a background paragraph. Review the strategies for writing introductory paragraphs and for selecting material for background paragraphs in Chapter 1, pages 29 and 37.

EXERCISE 13   Analyzing paragraphs

Review the following introductory and background paragraphs, and study the comments in the margin. Draw lines to connect the comments to the appropriate sections in the paragraphs. Then, with a partner, answer the questions that follow.

Report 1: Introductory and Background Paragraphs on AIDS

The introduction begins with some startling statistics.

Brief information about the topic is provided in two sentences.

The thesis statement presents the topic and the three controlling ideas.

The topic sentence includes the topic (background info about AIDS) and controlling ideas.

The Joint United Nations Programme on HIV/AIDS (UNAIDS) recently reported that over sixty million people have been infected with HIV since it was first diagnosed more than twenty years ago (TakingITGlobal, 2004). In addition, it is estimated that in the next twenty years, more than sixty-eight million people will die of AIDS. Acquired immune deficiency syndrome (AIDS) has become a serious problem that affects not only individuals and families but entire communities. This global problem must be addressed. To prevent the further spread of AIDS, it is important to understand the issues surrounding this disease, including its causes, prevention strategies, and consequences.

Some background information about AIDS is necessary to understand this disease and the issues that surround it. The media did not bring AIDS to the attention of the general public until the 1980s, but AIDS was actually discovered in the 1940s

A brief history of the disease is given.

Acronyms are provided after the full spelling of the terms.

Biological causes and process are briefly explained.

A quotation from a credible source is given with in-text citation (author, year, page #).

The paragraph ends with a concluding statement, not a quote or paraphrase.

This online article did not have an author, so it is alphabetized by the article title.

in Africa when the virus transferred from chimpanzees to humans (How, 1998). Scientists believe that the disease probably spread to the United States around 1968. Documented cases occurred in the early 1980s (Pearson, 2003). AIDS results from a viral infection, which is known as the human immunodeficiency virus (HIV). The greatest danger of HIV is that it hides inside healthy cells and then infects them, weakening their structure and ability to fight infection. A related problem is that patients do not show severe symptoms of AIDS right away. As stated in the college textbook *Biology Concepts and Applications*, "At first an infected person might appear to be in good health, suffering no more than a bout of the flu" (Starr, 2000, p. 578). However, when HIV is finally detected in a patient months or years later, the form of the virus can be quite different from the virus that first entered the body.

References

How AIDS Began. (1998, February). *The Economist*, 346, 81. Retrieved July 20, 2003, from EBSCO Host Research Databases (00130613).

Pearson, H. (2003, May 20). HIV's history traced. *Nature Science Update*. Retrieved July 14, 2003, from http://www.nature.com/nsu/030519/ 030519-2.html

Starr, C. (2000). *Biology concepts and applications* (4th ed.). New York: Brooks/Cole.

TakingITGlobal. (2004). *Understanding the issues: HIV/AIDS*. Retrieved April 12, 2004, from http://understanding.takingitglobal.org/health/HIVAIDS

Report 2: Introductory and Background Paragraphs on Anthrax

The introduction begins with a question that will be answered in the report.

Brief information is provided about the topic.

The thesis statement includes the topic and controlling ideas to be addressed.

In-text citation is used for both quotes and paraphrases.

The process of contracting the disease is explained.

Key terms are provided and defined.

Acronyms of credible sources are provided after the full spelling.

How dangerous is anthrax? The CDC (2004) categorizes anthrax as having "high bioterrorism potential." This means that anthrax has the potential of spreading, causing negative effects on the public's health. It also means that plans must be made to protect the public. For this reason, it is important to be educated about anthrax and to understand how anthrax is spread, what the symptoms are, and how it is treated.

The National Institute of Allergy and Infectious Diseases (NIAID) (2002) defines anthrax as "an acute infectious disease caused by the spore-forming, rod-shaped bacterium *Bacillus anthracis*" (para. 1). This disease comes from wild animals like cattle, sheep, goats, and other herbivores. Anthrax can lie dormant in the soil for many years. NIAID explains that after an animal eats the grass, the spores (reproductive organisms) are activated, and the bacteria reproduce, which can kill the infected animal. The bacteria of the dead animal then return to the soil or water again as spores, and the cycle continues. NIAID further reports that anthrax can be transmitted to humans when they eat or work with infected animals. A person with an open cut can contract the disease by touching infected animal hair, leather, or other animal products. This type of infection is known as cutaneous anthrax. With cutaneous anthrax, an itchy bump like an insect bite grows on the skin near the cut, but in one or two days, as the bacteria reproduce, a dark ulcer, or an infected sore, develops (CDC, 2004). The CDC also reports that early treatment with an antibiotic can cure anthrax. This is important, since according to the Occupational Safety and Health Administration (OSHA), approximately 20 percent of untreated cases of cutaneous anthrax will result in death (2004).

References

Centers for Disease Control and Prevention. (2004). *Anthrax: What you need to know.* Retrieved May 10, 2004, from http://www.bt.cdc.gov/agent/anthrax/needtoknow.asp

For online sources, include the date of the source (if available) and the date of retrieval. The "retrieval statement" should be: Retrieved month, day, year, from Web address. (Note: a period does not come after the Web address.)

National Institute of Allergy and Infectious Diseases. (2002, May). *Anthrax.* Retrieved May 26, 2004, from http://www.niaid.nih.gov/factsheets/anthrax.htm

Occupational Safety and Health Administration, U.S. Department of Labor. *Anthrax.* Retrieved May 16, 2004, from http://www.osha.gov/SLTC/etools/anthrax/disease_rec.html

1. How did the writer attempt to capture the readers' interest in Report 1? In Report 2? Examples may include a/an

   question   interesting, brief story
   fact/statistic   general, noncontroversial statement
   quotation   provocative, interesting statement
   definition

2. In each thesis statement, draw a box around the main topic and circle the controlling ideas.

3. How many body paragraphs do you expect to be developed in each

   report? Why? Report 1: ——————— Report 2: ———————

   _____

   _____

4. Based on the thesis statement, write two or three questions you expect to be answered in Report 1.

   _____

   _____

   _____

5. What factual and/or historical information about the disease is provided in Report 1?

   _____

   _____

6. In the background paragraph in Report 2, a quote is provided. Is the source of this quote credible? Why or why not?

_____

_____

SPOTLIGHT ON WRITING SKILLS

Defining

During your academic career, you will often need to *define* or explain new terms and ideas while you participate in class discussions and complete reading and writing assignments. When you read academic materials, find definitions and explanations of key terms and ideas that can help you understand the material. When you write academic assignments, include definitions and explanations to show your understanding of the material and to help your readers better understand your ideas.

Definitions of key terms often occur in the introductory and background paragraphs of academic papers because writers want to provide readers with basic information to understand the topic.

POWER GRAMMAR

Using Sentence-level Definitions with Key Terms

One way to include definitions in your writing is to provide sentence-level definitions. A *sentence-level definition* of a noun usually has three parts:

1. The term being defined
2. A verb (often *to be*: *is/are*)
3. A noun phrase that includes:
   a. The category the term belongs to
   b. Details that separate the term from other terms in the category

Term	is/are	Noun phrase	
		General category	**Specific details**
A virus	is	a microorganism	that causes diseases like the common cold, influenza, and measles.
Antibiotics	are	drugs	designed to fight bacterial infections.
A biochemist	is	a scientist	who studies the chemistry of living things.

noun phrase	
1. An epidemic is **a disease that spreads quickly among many people.**	The words that provide the specific details about the term are often in the form of a relative clause. If you need to review basic relative clause structure, go to the website for this book at http://esl.college.hmco.com/students. General category = a disease Specific details (relative clause) = that spreads quickly among many people
noun phrase	
2. Antibiotics are **drugs designed to fight bacterial infections.**	Sometimes the relative clause is reduced to leave just a past participle form of the verb. See the website for this book for more information on reduced relative clauses. General category = drugs Specific details (reduced relative clause) = (that are) designed to fight bacterial infections

EXERCISE 14 Writing sentence-level definitions

Review the sources you gathered and your information chart. Identify key terms you most likely will include and define in your chapter writing assignment. Then, write sentence-level definitions for your chosen disease and three other terms. Use both relative clauses and reduced relative clauses in your noun phrases.

Example

AIDS is a disease in which the body's immune system is unable to fight off certain infections.

1. _____

   _____

   _____

2. _____

   _____

   _____

3. _____

   _____

   _____

4. _____

   _____

   _____

POWER GRAMMAR

Using Definition Structures to Provide Key Terms and Definitions

In addition to a sentence-level definition, other structures can be used to provide definitions of important terms in your writing. The following table illustrates some of those structures.

Examples	Structures
1. Disease depends on relationships. Without both hosts (**the victims of bacteria**) and vectors (**the organisms that complete the chain of transmission**), microorganisms would not be able to reproduce and cause disease.	The definition is placed near the term and put in parentheses.
2. The influenza virus can make chronic medical situations, **like heart and lung illness,** worse.	The term is followed by examples that suggest a definition.
3. Noncommunicable diseases, **or diseases like cancer that originate in genetic or environmental factors,** are fast becoming the leading cause of disability and death.	The definition is included immediately after the term and set off from the term with commas + *or*.
4. There is little that doctors can do to treat SARS. Antibiotics, **drugs designed to treat bacterial infections,** do not appear to be effective.	The definition is set off from the term with commas.
5. Influenza—**an infectious respiratory disease that spreads through the air by coughing or sneezing**—infects more than 10 percent of the U.S. population annually.	The definition is set off from the term with dashes.

Examples	Structures
6. An epidemic affecting a very large area **is known as** a pandemic, and one that is consistently present in the population **is called** endemic.	The definition is given before the passive phrases *is called* and *is known as*.
7. Severe acute respiratory syndrome **is defined as** a viral illness that affects one's lungs and often causes pneumonia.	The definition is given after the passive phrase *is defined as*.
8. People infected with yellow fever showed symptoms like a high fever and jaundice, **which is yellow coloring of the skin caused by liver problems.**	The definition is provided as a non-restrictive relative clause.

EXERCISE 15 **Identifying definition structures**

Read the following paragraphs containing numerous definitions of key terms. In each paragraph, (a) underline the terms being defined, (b) circle the definition structures, including the verb to be, *and (c) place brackets around the definitions. Then, (d) draw an arrow to connect the term and its definition. One example is provided in Paragraph 1.*

1. <u>AIDS</u> (is) [a disease in which the body's immune system breaks down and is unable to fight off certain infections and other illnesses that take advantage of a weakened immune system.] When a person is infected with HIV, the virus enters the body and lives and multiplies primarily in the white blood cells—the immune cells that normally protect us from disease. The hallmark of HIV infection is the progressive loss of a specific type of immune cell, which is called T-helper or CD4 cells. As the virus reproduces, it damages or kills these and other cells, weakening the immune system and leaving the

individual vulnerable to various opportunistic infections, such as pneumonia and cancer.

Source: AMFAR AIDS Research. (2001). *Facts for life: What you and people you care about need to know about HIV/AIDS.* Retrieved April 12, 2004, from http://www.thebody.com/amfar/faq.html

2. Anthrax, a serious disease caused by *Bacillus anthracis*, which is a bacterium that forms spores, can occur in the skin, lungs, or digestive system. A bacterium is a very small organism made up of one cell. Many bacteria can cause disease. A spore is a cell that is dormant (asleep) but may come to life with the right conditions.

Source: Centers for Disease Control and Prevention. (2004). *Anthrax: What you need to know.* Retrieved May 10, 2004, from http://www.bt.cdc.gov/agent/anthrax/needtoknow.asp

☐ Drafting, Revising, and Editing

 EXERCISE 16 Planning and drafting your paragraphs

Draft your paragraphs by completing the following:

1. Draft an introductory paragraph that (a) stimulates your readers' interest, (b) provides brief information about your topic, and (c) includes a thesis statement. Your introduction might include key terms and their definitions.
2. Draft a background paragraph that includes factual and/or historical information about the disease you chose to write about. To choose which facts and information to include, review your essay map and information chart. Focus on the information that will help your readers understand your topic. You might also include key terms and their definitions.
3. Begin to draft a reference page that includes source information referred to or included in these paragraphs.
4. Save your writing in your notebook or folder or as a word-processed document.

EXERCISE 17 Revising your paragraphs

Before you ask others for feedback, review and revise your own writing:

1. Read your paragraphs carefully, and consider these questions:

   - Does your introduction stimulate your readers' interest, provide brief information, and include a thesis statement that has a topic and controlling ideas?
   - Does your background paragraph begin with a topic sentence that has a topic and controlling ideas?
   - In your background paragraph, have you adequately provided factual and/or historical information about the disease you chose to write about?
   - Should you provide more supporting information to help your audience better understand the disease?
   - Have you defined key terms related to your topic?
   - Have you explained the meaning of any acronyms included in your writing?
   - Have you included in-text citations when you used outside sources?
   - Have you used a variety of attribution signals with your paraphrases and quotes?
   - Have you explained the credibility of your sources?
   - Have you used cohesion devices to help your readers understand the connection of your ideas?

2. Make any changes needed to improve the meaning of your writing.
3. Save your revisions in your word-processed document, and print one copy of your paper.

EXERCISE 18 Providing and receiving peer feedback

Provide and receive feedback by completing the following:

1. Exchange papers with a partner, and read your partner's paragraphs. Do not hold a pen or pencil in your hand during this first reading.
2. Reread the paragraphs. This time, on your partner's paper, <u>underline</u> the thesis statement in the introductory paragraph.

3. In the margin, indicate how many body paragraphs you expect to be developed for this paper. Be ready to explain your opinion.
4. *Underline* the topic sentence in the background paragraph. In the margin of the background paragraph, write the type of supporting information used. For example, identify:

facts or statistics	expert opinions	descriptions
explanations	examples	personal experiences
observations		

5. Tell your partner what you like best about the writing. In the margin, write a statement like:

   These statistics are surprising and interesting.

   I like how you used different attribution signals in your writing.

   By reading your paper, I learned the causes of this disease.

6. Give one suggestion to improve your partner's writing. In the margin, write a statement like:

   I think you should add some more supporting information to better explain this idea.

   Can you provide a definition of this term?

   You need to include the source of this information.

7. Ask one question you have about the topic that was not answered in the paragraph. In the margin, write a question like:

   When was this disease first documented?

   What makes this person an expert on your topic?

   How many people are afflicted with this disease today?

8. Compare your partner's in-text citations to her or his reference page. Place a question mark (?) next to any potential problems.
9. With your partner, discuss your ideas and suggestions for her or his paper.

EXERCISE 19 Revising and editing your paragraphs

Improve your paragraphs by completing these steps:

1. Reread your paragraphs and consider the suggestions from your partner.
2. Make at least two or three changes to improve your writing.
3. Edit for grammar, punctuation, and spelling to reflect your best work.
4. Save your revisions in your word-processed document. Use this writing in your analytical report. Your instructor may also want to collect your writing for review or evaluation.

> **Master Student Tip**
>
> ▼ Save a copy of each draft you write, whether a paragraph or a whole essay. Choose *Save As* and rename the file (such as *AIDS Draft 2*) so that a new document is created. After you complete your final draft, you can review the progression your writing has taken and apply the processes you have learned to future assignments. Also, your instructor may require early drafts to be turned in with your final report.

SPOTLIGHT ON WRITING SKILLS

Quoting and Paraphrasing

Most academic writing assignments require you to research a topic and present information from your research. *Quoting* and *paraphrasing* are important techniques used by academic writers to include information from outside sources in their papers. (See Chapter 1, p. 28, and Appendixes 1-2 for more information.)

When you quote, you copy others' ideas exactly and put quotation marks around the words. You also include in-text citation (the author's last name, year of publication, and page/paragraph number of original quote).

Example

In his article, Sinnott (2004) declared, "There are diseases we cannot know are incubating, ready to break out. I worry not just that we will see more, but that their severity will increase" (p. 15).

When you paraphrase, you restate others' ideas in your own words. That is, you write the meaning of the author's ideas. You use some of the author's key terms, but you use many of your own words and sentence structures. You also include in-text citation, including the author's last name and the year of publication.

Example

Sinnott (2004) expressed his concern that the future may bring diseases that are even more severe than what we have experienced to date.

Although you can occasionally use a direct quotation in your writing, one convention of academic writing is to paraphrase more frequently than quoting.

Follow these steps when paraphrasing:

1. Select a short passage (about one to four sentences) that supports an idea in your paper.
2. Read the passage carefully to fully understand it.
3. Take notes about the main idea and supporting points you think you should include in the paraphrase. Include keywords and terms used by the author.
4. Using only your notes, write a paraphrase. Your paraphrase should be about the same length as the original source.
5. Reread the original source. Is there important information that you have forgotten or written inaccurately? Is your paraphrase too similar to the original source? If so, revise your paraphrase.
6. Add in-text citation if you have not already done so.

POWER GRAMMAR

Using Your Own Words in Paraphrases

Following are some techniques you can use to help you paraphrase. An effective paraphrase includes <u>more than one</u> of these techniques. If you use only one of these techniques when paraphrasing, you have not paraphrased effectively.

1. <u>Change a word form from one part of speech to another.</u>
   Original: Medical professor John Swanson says that global changes are influencing the spread of disease.
   Paraphrase: According to John Swanson, a professor of medicine, changes across the globe are causing diseases to spread (James, 2004).

Original	Paraphrase
medical professor	professor of medicine
global changes	changes across the globe
the spread of disease	diseases to spread

2. Use synonyms.

Original: The U.S. government declared that the AIDS crisis poses a national security threat. The announcement followed an intelligence report that found that high rates of HIV infection could lead to widespread political destabilization.

Paraphrase: The government of the United States announced that AIDS could harm the nation's security. The government warned the population after an important governmental study concluded that political problems could result from large numbers of people infected with HIV (Snell, 2005).

Original	Paraphrase
declared	announced
an intelligence report	a governmental study
found	concluded
high rates	large numbers of people
political destabilization	political problems

3. Change numbers and percentages to different forms.

Original: Minority groups in the United States have been hit hardest by the epidemic. African Americans, who made up 13 percent of the U.S. population, accounted for 46 percent of the AIDS cases diagnosed in 1998.

Paraphrase: The AIDS epidemic has mostly affected minorities in the United States. For example, in 1998, less than 15 percent of the total population was African American, but almost half of the people diagnosed with AIDS in the United States that year were African American (Jenson, 2000).

Original	Paraphrase
13 percent of the U.S. population	less than 15 percent of the total population
46 percent of the AIDS cases	almost half of the people diagnosed with AIDS

4. Change the word order (e.g., change from active to passive and vice versa, move modifiers to different positions).
    Original: Angier (2001) reported that malaria kills more than one million people annually, the overwhelming majority of them children in sub-Saharan Africa.
    Paraphrase: Every year, more than a million people are killed by malaria, and most of the victims are children who live in sub-Saharan Africa (Angier, 2001).

Original	Paraphrase
annually	every year
malaria kills more than one million people	more than a million people are killed by malaria

5. Use different definition structures.
    Original: Lyme disease is an inflammatory disease caused by a bacterium transmitted by ticks (small bloodsucking arachnids that attach themselves to larger animals). The disease is usually characterized by a rash followed by flu-like symptoms, including fever, joint pain, and headache.
    Paraphrase: Lyme disease—a disease that causes swelling and redness—is caused by a bacterium carried by a small arachnid known as a tick. The ticks attach to and suck the blood of animals and humans. As a tick bites, it transfers some of the Lyme disease bacteria into the animal or human. The symptoms of Lyme disease include a fever, pains in the joints, and a headache (Wald, 2005).

Original	Paraphrase
Lyme disease is an inflammatory disease	Lyme disease—a disease that causes swelling and redness
ticks (small bloodsucking arachnids)	a small arachnid known as a tick

6. Use different attribution signals.
   Original: "That's because there are so many different ways the disease could have arrived," veterinarian Mark Walters declared in his recent book, *Six Modern Plagues*.
   Paraphrase: According to Mark Walters, a veterinarian who wrote *Six Modern Plagues*, the disease could have arrived in numerous ways (Peterson, 2004).

Original	Paraphrase
Mark Walters declared	According to Mark Walters,

7. Change the sentence structure, and use different connecting words.
   Original: Although only about one-tenth of the world population lives there, sub-Saharan Africa remains the hardest-hit region, accounting for 72 percent of the people infected with HIV during 2000.
   Paraphrase: Approximately 10 percent of the world's population reside in sub-Saharan Africa. However, this area of the world has the highest percentage of AIDS-related illnesses. In fact, in 2000, almost three-fourths of the population had the HIV virus (Bunting, 2004).

Original	Paraphrase
Although ..., sub-Saharan Africa remains the hardest-hit region ...	... population reside in sub-Saharan Africa. However, ...
..., accounting for 72 percent of the people ...	In fact, in 2000, almost three fourths of the population ...

8. <u>Do not change key terms or proper nouns.</u>
   Original: In the northeastern United States, people are building homes on the edge of woods, where the ticks that carry Lyme disease hitch rides on deer. In addition, in Africa, hunters bring back the meat of animals that scientists think may transmit Ebola, a usually fatal virus that causes massive hemorrhaging in its victims.
   Paraphrase: In the United States, residential areas are being built near wooded areas in the northeast. These areas are also the homes of ticks carrying Lyme disease. Also, according to scientists, hunters in Africa kill animals that may carry the Ebola virus (an often fatal virus that causes massive hemorrhaging) (Yaya, 2004).

Original	Paraphrase
ticks that carry Lyme disease	ticks carrying Lyme disease
in Africa	in Africa
Ebola	the Ebola virus
massive hemorrhaging	massive hemorrhaging

EXERCISE 20 **Identifying paraphrasing techniques**

Read the following passages and their paraphrases. For each item, words and phrases from the original passage are listed in a chart. Identify similar ideas in the paraphrase, and write the words and phrases in the chart. Examples are provided for the first passage.

1. **Original:** In the fourteenth century, Latin Christendom was afflicted with an agricultural crisis. Limited use of fertilizers and limited knowledge of conservation exhausted the topsoil. From 1301 to 1314, there was a general shortage of food, and from 1315 to 1317, famine struck Europe. Throughout the country, malnutrition was widespread.

   Source: Perry, M., Baker, J.W., & Hollinger, P. (2003). *The humanities in the western tradition.* Boston: Houghton Mifflin.

Paraphrase: According to Perry, Baker, and Hollinger (2003), agricultural problems were the major cause of starvation in early fourteenth-century Europe. For example, farmers did not use much fertilizer and did not understand how to conserve topsoil. These practices led to severe food shortages and widespread suffering throughout Europe, including starvation.

Original	Paraphrase
in the fourteenth century, Latin Christendom	*in early fourteenth-century Europe*
limited use of fertilizers	
limited knowledge of conservation	
a general shortage of food	
was widespread	*widespread suffering*
malnutrition	

2. **Original:** Although microbes have always had the traveling bug, in centuries past, it took at least a few weeks or months for sailors to deliver a ship of rats bearing fleas with bubonic-plague bacteria from the Orient to Europe. Nowadays, a mosquito infested with the malaria parasite can be buzzing in Ghana at dawn and dining on an airport employee in Boston by cocktail hour.

Source: Angier, N. (2001). Together, in sickness and in health. *Global politics in a changing world* (2nd ed.). Boston: Houghton Mifflin.

Paraphrase: In the past, bacterial infections, such as the bubonic plague, spread gradually from one continent to another due to slow travel by ships. However, in the present time, a malaria-infected mosquito can travel from Africa to America in just one day (Angier, 2001).

Original	Paraphrase
in centuries past	
bubonic-plague bacteria	
from the Orient to Europe	
nowadays	
mosquito infested with the malaria parasite	
buzzing in Ghana at dawn and dining on an airport employee in Boston by cocktail hour	

3. **Original:** In the past week, country after country has admitted that millions of birds and a few people have succumbed to bird flu, and it has become clear that we are facing the worst-ever outbreak of the disease. A combination of official cover-up and questionable farming practices allowed the bird flu outbreak to turn into the epidemic now under way.

   Source: NewScientist.com. (2004, January 28). *Bird flu outbreak started a year ago.* Retrieved April 13, 2004, from http://www.newscientist.com/news/news.jsp?id=ns99994614

   Paraphrase: As reported on NewScientist.com (2004), numerous countries have recently acknowledged that millions of birds (and some people) have died as a result of contracting bird flu. The website explains that we can now say that the disease has the potential of causing major public health complications across the world. In fact, the result of the denial of a potential problem by public officials, along with the practices of local farmers, has led to an epidemic.

Original	Paraphrase
in the past week	
country after country has admitted	
have succumbed to bird flu	
we are facing the worst-ever outbreak of the disease	
official cover-up	

EXERCISE 21 **Paraphrasing supporting information**

The information in the following passages might be used as supporting information in a student's report. Learn more about paraphrasing by completing the following:

Read each passage, and write a paraphrase on separate paper. Follow the steps and techniques for paraphrasing discussed previously, and use at least four or five different techniques. In addition, use in-text citation in your paraphrases.

1. **Original:** The situation regarding HIV/AIDS in Southern Africa goes far beyond a food shortage that will pass with the next harvest. HIV/ AIDS has turned what was already a complex emergency into a crisis on a massive scale—a crisis that will have a lasting impact across the region for years to come. The eyes of the world may be focusing elsewhere, but Southern Africa needs our attention now more than ever.

   Source: *Oxfam community aid abroad: Aids and hunger*. Retrieved April 13, 2004, from http://www.caa.org.au/pr/2002/aidsandhunger.html

2. **Original:** Monkeypox is a rare viral disease that occurs mostly in central and western Africa. It is called "monkeypox" because it was first found in 1958 in laboratory monkeys. Blood tests of animals in Africa later found that other types of animals probably had monkeypox, including squirrels, rats, mice, and rabbits. Monkeypox was reported in humans for the first time in 1970.

   Source: Centers for Disease Control and Prevention. (2003, June 12). *Fact sheet: What you should know about monkeypox*. Retrieved April 14, 2004, from http://www.cdc.gov/ncidod/monkeypox/factsheet2.htm

3. **Original:** According to Harry Balzer, vice president of the market-information company The NPD Group, issues such as terrorist threats, foodborne-illness outbreaks, and mad cow discoveries tend to have little impact on overall confidence regarding food safety. A study done by the Reed Research Group supports this theory, with 53 percent of consumers reporting that they are very confident in the safety of beef in the United States.

Source: Perlik, A. (2004, March 1). *How now, mad cow?* Keepmedia.com. Retrieved April 14, 2004, from http://www.keepmedia.com/ShowItemDetails.do;jsessionid=agTZNYDD2i2-?nbdTopicID=49&item_id=387682

Exchange paraphrases with a classmate, and complete the following:

1. Underline the main ideas and key supporting points in each original passage, and identify them in the paraphrase. If you cannot locate a main idea or key supporting point in the paraphrase, write the idea in the margin of the paraphrase.
2. Look back at the original texts if you disagree with the accuracy of your classmate's paraphrases, and write a question mark (?) next to your concerns in the margin of the paraphrase.
3. At the bottom of each paraphrase, indicate two or three paraphrasing techniques that were used (e.g., word form, sentence structure, synonym).
4. Compare the length of your partner's paraphrases to the original texts. They should be about the same length. If they are not, write a note about the length in the margin.
5. Review your partner's use of in-text citation. In the margin, write any questions you have about the use of citation.
6. In your opinion, are your partner's paraphrases effective? Why or why not?
7. Return your partner's paraphrases, and discuss your comments and questions.

 EXERCISE 22   Planning and drafting your body paragraphs

Plan and draft your body paragraphs for your report. Remember, your body paragraphs should analyze and explain the causes, reasons, effects, and other factors related to your topic.

Master Student Tip

It is important to review the details of your assignment throughout the writing process to ensure that you address the assignment.

1. To begin, review the chapter writing assignment and look at your essay map, information chart, and introductory and background paragraphs.
2. Review the sample student report provided in Exercise 3. Notice the topic sentences for each of this student's body paragraphs.
3. Use the skills you have practiced to develop two or three body paragraphs for your own report. Specifically, include the following:

   - Definitions of key terms
   - Cohesion devices to help your readers understand the connection of your ideas
   - Paraphrases from at least two to four outside sources
   - Appropriate in-text citation with a variety of attribution signals
   - Information to explain the credibility of your sources

4. Add all outside source information to your reference page.
5. Add and save your body paragraphs to your word-processed document. Your instructor may also want to collect your paragraphs for review or evaluation.

EXERCISE 23 Analyzing a concluding paragraph

Read the following concluding paragraph written for a student report on influenza. Study the comments in the margin. Then, with a partner, answer the questions that follow.

Student Sample: Concluding Paragraph on Influenza

The paragraph begins with a general, noncontroversial statement.

The main ideas discussed in the body paragraphs are restated.

The paragraph ends with a recommendation.

In brief, although influenza itself is not a deadly disease, people should not underestimate this virus. The flu can cause some deadly complications. Flu shots are not 100 percent effective in preventing the flu because the strains of the flu viruses change from year to year. In addition, there is no drug to cure influenza. The medicines that infected people take can only alleviate the symptoms of the flu. Thus, people should maintain good habits in their daily life, such as exercising frequently and eating a balanced diet. An overall healthy lifestyle strengthens the immune system and resistance to disease. In short, people need to avoid catching the flu and spreading the flu virus to others.

1. What strategy (e.g., quotation, brief story, statistic) did the writer use to begin the concluding paragraph?
2. After reading this conclusion, what main ideas do you expect were developed in the essay?
3. How did the writer end the concluding paragraph?

EXERCISE 24 **Planning and drafting your conclusion**

Write your paragraph by completing these steps:

1. Read your entire report once more to prepare to write the conclusion.
2. Consider the strategy you used in your introductory paragraph and decide what strategy would be effective to begin your concluding paragraph.
3. Identify and summarize two or three main ideas from your report that you will refer to in the conclusion.
4. Decide what final comments you can offer on the topic, but do not introduce new information.
5. Draft your concluding paragraph.
6. Add and save the conclusion to your word-processed document.

EXERCISE 25 **Revising your analytical report**

To make sure that you have adequately fulfilled the requirements of the assignment, review the chapter writing assignment again. Then, slowly and thoughtfully reread your entire report. Make revisions where appropriate. Review your reference page to be sure all sources used when writing your report are included. Use the format of the reference page in Appendix 3, "End-of-Text References." Print a copy of your report.

EXERCISE 26 **Providing and receiving peer feedback**

Work with a partner, and exchange copies of your analytical report. Review your partner's report. To offer feedback to your partner, use the "Final Peer Review Sheet" located on this book's website at http://esl.college.hmco.com/students. Return and discuss your partner's paper.

EXERCISE 27 Finalizing your report

Finalize your report by completing the following:

1. Consider your partner's suggestions and your own insights as you revise your report.
2. Edit for grammar, spelling, and punctuation to reflect your best work.
3. Save the document as your final draft, and print one copy.
4. Attach your draft(s) and copies of all outside sources referred to while writing your report.
5. Submit your paper and attachments for your instructor's review and evaluation.

☐ More Practice and Self-Assessment

1. Return to the objectives at the beginning of this chapter. Read each objective, and put a check mark in the appropriate box: "I have learned this well" or "I need to work on this." Compare your responses to similar ones in Chapter 1. Has your understanding of certain writing skills improved since the previous chapter? Why or why not? Share your objectives chart with your instructor.
2. Write a paragraph explaining how to complete an analytical report with recommendations to other students who will complete this assignment. What methods work best? Why?
3. With a classmate, answer these questions about a reference page.
   a. Where do you put your reference list?
   b. In what order should your sources be listed?
   c. Describe the left margin of a reference list.
   d. For a book source, how is the book title capitalized?
   e. For a newspaper article source, how are both the article and the newspaper titles indicated?
   f. For a Web source, what date(s) is/are included?

WEB POWER

You can find additional exercises related to the content in this chapter at http://esl.college.hmco.com/students.

Writing a Persuasive Essay

Many academic assignments require you to write an essay that not only explains a topic but also asks you to form an opinion and support that opinion. The result is that you persuade (convince) your readers to share your opinion. To persuade effectively, express your opinion clearly and then provide strong support (evidence) for that opinion.

Persuasive writing comes in many forms, including newspaper editorials, restaurant or movie reviews, advertisements, and academic papers.

Chapter Objectives

Read the following chapter objectives to preview the chapter content. After you complete the chapter, return to this chart and check (✓) the appropriate boxes on the right.	I have learned this well.	I need to work on this.
Follow a 3-step writing process to gather, organize, and draft information		
Complete online "advanced searches"		
Develop library research skills		
Practice active reading strategies		
Interview an expert to collect information		
Construct an information chart to synthesize information		
Understand essay development for persuasive papers		
Create an essay map to organize information		
Write a thesis statement of opinion		
Form and support opinions		
Use language to control the strength of an opinion		
Understand degrees of plagiarism		
Practice summary writing		
Cite sources (in-text and end-of-text references)		

Chapter Writing Assignment

You will investigate online learning: learning that takes place through computers, not in classrooms, with computers linking the instructor and students electronically. First, you will consider what characteristics (i.e., qualities, features) help learning in a traditional classroom. Then, you will analyze whether two of those characteristics can also contribute to online learning. This assignment requires you to complete Internet and library research and interview an expert.

Your three- to four-page paper should be both informative and persuasive. Your purposes are to (a) educate your readers about online learning and (b) persuade them to share the conclusions you reach. Your essay must include the following:

- An introductory paragraph with a thesis statement of opinion
- A background paragraph that includes factual, descriptive, and/or historical information about online learning
- Two or three body paragraphs that:
  a. Describe and explain the features of successful classroom learning
  b. Provide your opinion about the contribution of those qualities in an online learning environment
  c. Support your opinion with facts, examples, experience, and evidence from authorities
- A concluding paragraph
- At least two to four in-text citations
- An end-of-text reference page with references for all sources referred to as you wrote your essay

To complete your persuasive essay, you will employ the three-step writing process:

1. Gathering Information
2. Focusing and Organizing
3. Drafting, Revising, and Editing

☐ Gathering Information

EXERCISE 1 Discussing and writing about online learning

Even if you have not experienced learning online, you probably have some ideas about online classes and some opinions about the differences between classroom learning and online learning. Discuss and share your ideas about online learning with a small group of classmates. Then, for five minutes, write everything you can think of that relates to online learning. Include what you consider advantages and disadvantages of online learning, and write questions you have about online classes. Save your writing in a notebook or folder for future reference.

EXERCISE 2 Reading about and discussing online education

Read the following paragraph, and review the comments about paragraph organization provided in the margin. Then, with your instructor and classmates, discuss the questions that follow. Take notes of your discussion, and save your notes in your writing notebook or folder for future reference.

Student Paragraph: Online Education

The topic sentence introduces the main idea (online education) and controlling idea (positive changes). →

An example illustrates positive change (easy, fast communication). →

Another positive change is provided (interesting terms for courses). →

Online or distance education is not a new concept in the U.S. higher educational system, but distance courses have changed in positive ways over the past decades. The original "correspondence course" is now out of date. Students and instructors do not send packages of exercises and writing assignments in the mail and wait three weeks for answers anymore. Instead, they use the Internet for easy and fast communication 24 hours a day. Even the terminology that institutions use to describe their online education courses sounds convenient and inviting. For example, on the Internet homepages of universities around the country, links to online courses attract students with modern names like "open campus," "Web courses," and "e-learning." Most college websites also provide basic information about online education so that interested students can easily decide whether this type of instruction will suit them.

Specific details are ⟶
included
(characteristics of
online learning).

A credible source is ⟶
included.

The concluding ⟶
sentence makes a
future prediction.

Some common characteristics of online education include
(1) the separation of instructor and learner in space and/or
time, (2) the use of technology to deliver course content and to
connect learners to resources, (3) two-way communication tools
between instructor and learner, and (4) control of learning by the
student (Johnson, 2005). These characteristics present many
exciting challenges to online course designers, instructors, and
their students. As advances in and access to technology
continually improve e-learning, this type of instruction will
certainly continue to evolve and grow more popular in the
twenty-first century.

Reference

Johnson, J. (2005). Emerging e-learning. *Journal of Instructional
Technology, 55,* 48–51.

1. What is online learning?
2. What terms are used to refer to online education?
3. Have you or someone you know taken an online course? If so,
   briefly describe the course and what was learned.
4. In your opinion, what are the advantages of online courses?
5. What do you think are the disadvantages of online courses?

 EXERCISE 3 **Analyzing a body paragraph**

*Read this body paragraph from an essay about online communication tools,
and study the comments in the margin. Then, with a partner, complete and
discuss the questions that follow. Take notes of your discussion, and save
your notes for future reference.*

Body Paragraph: Communication Tools

The first communication tool (course-discussion area) and descriptive details about its use are provided.

A second communication tool (e-mail) and descriptive details about its use are provided.

A third communication tool (chatroom) and descriptive details are provided.

Readers are guided from one tool to the next with <u>cohesion devices</u>.

Electronic communication tools provide many opportunities for students and faculty to engage in frequent and meaningful "conversation." <u>One</u> of the most common ways students keep in contact with their instructors and classmates is by using the course-discussion area. This tool provides students with a place to write their thoughts and ask questions, as well as to read what other students have to say. <u>Another</u> form of communication is e-mail, which is available 24 hours a day, so students can always send messages to their instructor. The instructor can also send e-mail to the class concerning, for example, a change in a reading assignment or the due date of an essay. <u>Finally</u>, one of the most popular electronic communication tools is the chatroom, where students can "talk" in real time with their classmates. Even those students who cannot log on for a chat can access the instant messages later if the instructor saves the text in a file.

1. Underline the topic sentence, and circle the controlling idea(s).

2. Draw lines from the controlling idea(s) to the information about each in the paragraph.

3. Discuss the forms of electronic communication described in the paragraph that you have used or are familiar with.

4. In your opinion, do the electronic communication tools described in the paragraph offer as many opportunities for forming a "community of students" as traditional classroom opportunities do? Briefly explain your opinion.

5. In your opinion, (a) will some students find it easier to communicate through the computer than in a traditional classroom? (b) If so, what kinds of students? (c) Why might they find the computer an easier form of communication?

 EXERCISE 4 Listing learning features

With a small group of students, complete a list of about ten features that help students learn effectively and successfully in a classroom. (Each group member should write a list.) Here are a few suggestions.

CHARACTERISTICS OF AN EFFECTIVE CLASSROOM LEARNING ENVIRONMENT

1. Students feel free to ask questions when they do not understand the materials.
2. Assignments are carefully explained so that students can complete them.
3. Students feel comfortable—physically and emotionally—in class.

Share your group's list with your class. Add new ideas from your classmates to your own list. (Your list should now have 15 to 20 characteristics.) Put your list in your writing notebook or folder. You will refer to this list when you write your essay.

SPOTLIGHT ON WRITING SKILLS

Forming and Expressing Opinions

In a persuasive essay, you must form an opinion about your topic. For this essay, you select and investigate two qualities that contribute to an effective classroom learning environment. You then form an opinion about whether those features can be successfully incorporated into an online course.

To analyze the qualities you select, ask "can" questions to focus your research. Here are some examples of "can" questions for the sample characteristics listed in Exercise 4.

1. Can students easily ask questions and promptly receive answers to questions in an online course?
2. Can instructors carefully explain e-learning assignments so that students can complete them confidently and successfully?
3. Can students in e-courses feel comfortable—physically and emotionally—in an online course?

Here are some other questions that students have asked while completing this chapter's writing assignment.

4. Can online courses lead to class discussions of the same quality as those in a traditional classroom?
5. Can e-course students develop a sense of community like students do on campus?
6. Can online learners receive prompt, effective feedback on their assignments?
7. Can students in e-courses have the same quality and amount of contact with their instructor as they can in a traditional classroom?

Answers to these kinds of questions, whether positive or negative, will help you draft your "working" thesis statement for your essay.

EXERCISE 5 Considering your topic

Determine the focus of your essay by completing these steps:

1. Consult your list of characteristics of an effective learning environment from Exercise 4. Select four qualities that you think are possible choices for your essay.
2. Write a "can" question for each quality.
3. Share your "can" questions with a partner. Ask your partner's advice about which two characteristics are more interesting and appropriate (and ask why).
4. Consider using those two qualities for your essay.

EXERCISE 6 Discussing your topic

Continue to gather information for your essay by following these steps:

1. With your partner, join another pair of peers. Share your "can" questions about effective learning features, and discuss them in relation to an online learning environment.
2. With the help of your classmates, complete a "yes/no chart" like the following example for at least two of your selected learning characteristics.

"Can students easily ask questions and receive prompt answers in an online learning course?"	
Yes, because . . .	**No, because . . .**
1. Students can e-mail questions to their instructor anytime, 24–7.	1. No instructor is available 24–7.
2. The instructor can explain that he or she will reply to all questions within 24 hours.	2. Students may not feel comfortable waiting 24 hours for a reply.
3. The instructor can show students how to "flag" an important question that needs immediate attention.	3. The instructor may not check e-mail hourly.

3. Save your yes/no charts in your writing folder or notebook for later use. Your instructor may also want to collect your chart for review or evaluation.

SPOTLIGHT ON WRITING SKILLS

Online Advanced Searches

For this chapter's writing assignment, you research two qualities that contribute to successful classroom learning. Then, you analyze whether those characteristics can (or cannot) contribute to an online learning environment. Your research will lead you to form opinions and draw conclusions about how well online courses meet students' needs.

The Internet is a logical place to research online learning. However, when you use online search engines, you often locate many more websites and articles than you can read, and many of those websites are not directly related to your topic. For instance, typing in the phrase or keywords "time on task" in Google produces over ten million items (*hits*)!

To find information that closely matches your keywords, perform an *Advanced Search*. The Advanced Search option in online search engines allows you to search efficiently for specific topics. To see how effective the Advanced Search option can be, look at this sample. The student used the following process to find specific information about her selected characteristic of effective classroom learning. (If you are at a computer, you can follow these steps and compare answers.)

"Can faculty and students maintain good contact in online courses?"

1. She opened Google.com and clicked the Advanced Search button.
2. She typed "faculty student contact" into the first box, labeled "Find results with <u>all</u> of the words."
3. She clicked Google Search.
   a. 6,080,000 items (*hits*) were found.
   b. The subject heading (the name of a link) in the first item was "News results for faculty student contact."
   c. The first page of results had three hits that contained the complete phrase "faculty student contact"—not just one or two of the words.
4. After the student located and read information on several of the websites, she clicked the Back button to return to the Google Advanced Search page. This time, she:
   a. Typed "faculty student contact" into the box labeled "Find results with the <u>exact</u> phrase"

b. Clicked Google Search
  - 1,510 hits were found.
  - The subject heading (the name of a link) in the first item was "College student inventory faculty student contact form."
  - The first page of results had seven hits that contained the exact phrase "faculty student contact."

The websites the student found by choosing the exact phrase option in this Advanced Search helped her focus and complete her online research for her essay.

Similar to the work of this student, the Advanced Search option on Google (or another search engine) can help you focus and find information about your selected characteristics. First, however, you must select keywords—phrases to type into search boxes—that describe your learning features. Here are some keywords that students selected about their features for effective learning:

Features	Keywords
collaborative problem-solving	student collaborative problem solving
sense of community	student learning community
learn in individual ways	diverse learning styles
access to instructor	students access instructor

EXERCISE 7 Performing an Advanced Search

Follow the process described previously as you perform an Advanced Search in Google.

1. Open Google and choose the Advanced Search option.
2. Choose keywords for one of your chosen features.
3. Type your keyword phrase into the first search box, "Find results with all the words."
4. Select several websites to visit, and print information that relates to your essay.
5. Return to the Advanced Search page.
6. Type your keyword phrase into the next box, "Find results with the exact phrase."
7. Select several websites to visit, and print information that relates to your essay.
8. Repeat the steps for your other chosen feature.

Master Student Tip

When you gather information for an academic paper, do not limit yourself to the Internet. Libraries have materials you cannot access on the Web, and trained librarians can assist you in your search for information.

EXERCISE 8 Completing library research

Visit your college library. Locate the computerized card catalog to begin your search for materials. Use your keywords to identify library materials. Find four or five sources of information during this visit. Ask a librarian for help if needed. (See Chapter 2, p. 59, for more information about using libraries and their extensive databases.)

SPOTLIGHT ON WRITING SKILLS

Interviewing an Expert

Another way to collect information about an academic topic is to interview an authority. Through interviews, you can gather statistics for your introductory and background paragraphs, as well as information and viewpoints for the body of your paper.

In most cases, prepare your questions in advance of your interview so that you can gather the information you need and be efficient and organized.

For this chapter writing assignment, you interview either an online instructor or a student who is taking or has taken an online course. Following are some questions you might choose to ask your "expert." Note that in some questions, you need to insert the qualities of learning environments that you are investigating.

Sample Interview Questions (Instructor)

1. How long have you been teaching? How long have you been teaching online?
2. How did you learn to teach online? Do you think special skills are needed? Should any instructor who is beginning online teaching learn special skills?
3. What motivated you to try teaching online? Why have you continued?
4. Have you ever been a student in an online course? If so, did you like it? Why or why not?
5. Do you think online instructors should learn online before they teach online? Why or why not?

6. Do you enjoy teaching online as much as you enjoy classroom teaching? Why or why not?
7. In what ways do you modify your classroom courses when you teach online? Which of these modifications do you think are most important? Why?
8. What course tools are most important for you to teach well online?
9. How many hours per week do you typically spend preparing for, delivering, and interacting with students in your online course? How does that compare with your work in a traditional classroom course?
10. Are online students different from classroom students? If so, in what specific ways?
11. Do you see a similar amount of learning and improvement in online students as in classroom students?
12. What special challenges can online courses present for (a) instructors and (b) students?
13. Some research indicates that online students drop classes more than traditional classroom students do. In your experience, has this been true? If so, can you offer any reasons? What have you done to increase retention of online students?
14. What advice do you give students to help them successfully complete your online course(s)?
15. What advice would you give an instructor who is thinking about teaching an online course?
16. Which of the following online techniques do you use in your online courses, and how would you rate the effectiveness of each?
    a. monitored discussion area (bulletin board)
    b. posted notes and study guides on the site
    c. multimedia presentations (e.g., slides)
    d. posted readings and other materials
    e. e-mail
    f. streaming videotape
    g. links to other websites
    h. online quizzes/tests

17. Which of the following classroom teaching characteristics do you think are (a) better, (b) the same, or (c) less effective or possible in online courses?
    a. student participation
    b. student-instructor communication
    c. meeting diverse student needs
    d. feedback to students
    e. sense of "community"
    f. STUDENT: insert your selected qualities

Sample Interview Questions (Student)

1. How many courses have you taken online?

2. Have you completed every course you began? If not, why not?

3. Why did you decide to take your first online course?

4. How do you think the effectiveness of your online instructors compare with the effectiveness of traditional classroom instructors? Consider such qualities as:
    a. prompt feedback on exercises and tests
    b. presentation of course materials
    c. interaction with students
    d. overall preparation
    e. STUDENT: insert your selected qualities

5. What online teaching techniques do you like most? Least? Why? Consider such techniques as:
    a. links to other sources of materials
    b. postings to discussion area
    c. media files
    d. streaming videotape
    e. STUDENT: insert your selected qualities

6. What did you like best about the online format of the class? Why? What did you like least? Why?

7. Do you think you learned (a) less, (b) the same amount, or (c) more course material in your online class as compared with traditional classroom courses?

8. What do you think caused you to have that opinion?

9. Do you think online instructors should learn special teaching techniques before they teach online? Why or why not? If so, what should they learn?

10. How many hours per week did you typically spend online for a single course? Do you think you spend a comparable amount of time on a traditional classroom course? Why or why not?

EXERCISE 9 Locating and interviewing an expert

Complete these steps to locate and interview an expert:

1. Identify (a) an instructor who teaches online courses or (b) a student who is taking or has taken an online course. Ask your instructor and classmates for advice on identifying "experts." You may also locate an online instructor by looking on your college website under Distance Education Courses.

2. Contact your expert and ask to make an appointment to talk about her or his experiences as an online instructor or student. (You may interview the expert face-to-face or arrange to interview by e-mail or telephone.)

3. Prepare a list of your interview questions, selected from the previous examples. Select only those questions that will help you with your chapter writing assignment. (Limit your questions to use no more than 20 minutes of the expert's time.)

4. Complete the interview with the expert. To clarify a point during the interview, ask about it immediately; interviewees want the facts to be accurate. You might say:

"Did you say that . . .?"

"I'm sorry. I didn't quite understand. Could you please repeat your answer."

"Am I correct in thinking that you agree with X about . . .?"

5. Record the expert's name and the date of your interview. You will need this citation information when you write your essay.

Supporting Opinions

For any academic persuasive paper, strong support is essential. As you reread the information you have gathered from the Internet, library, and interviewee(s), highlight, underline, or photocopy relevant supporting material (like facts, authoritative quotations, and research results). This supporting information will strengthen your opinions and persuade your readers.

Here are examples of support for some qualities of successful clasroom learning that are also effective in online learning.

Ways to support opinions	Examples
Facts and statistics	Electronic storage capacity permits students to save important information and easily retrieve this material when needed (Gilbert, 2004).
Examples	For example, the flexibility of online courses provides access to a college education for many students who cannot attend classes on the campus (Singer, 2003).
Experts	According to William Patten (2005), an online instructor of professional writing, one strength of teaching through the computer is that students write more (because they cannot "speak").
Research results	As reported by Anderson (2004), students with reflective, analytic learning styles are empowered by the extra time to think before they reply during class "discussions" on the computer.
Interviews	Mana Yamamoto, a student who has taken four online courses, says she prefers learning through the computer because she can choose the best time to do her work (M. Yamamoto, personal communication, January 8, 2005).

EXERCISE 10 Identifying supporting information

Collect and review your notes, your yes/no charts, and the information you gathered from your online, library, and interview sources. Highlight (or circle or underline) any information you think you will use for your first selected quality of a successful classroom. With another highlighter color (or another form of identification, such as circling or underlining), mark any information you think you will use for your second selected feature.

☐ Focusing and Organizing

EXERCISE 11 Organizing your information

Organize the information you have collected by completing the following:

1. Use four sheets of paper to divide your information into paragraphs. At the top of each sheet, write one part of an essay (introduction, background, body paragraphs, and conclusion). Here is an example of the introduction information page.

┌─────────────────────┐
│ Introduction   │
│   │
│   │
│   │
│   │
│   │
└─────────────────────┘

2. Review the information you gathered for your essay. Write the highlighted (or circled or underlined) information on the appropriate page. Include source information, such as the author's or expert's name and the source date.
3. Save your pages in your notebook or folder for future use. Your instructor may also want to collect your pages for review or evaluation.

Essay Maps and Thesis Statements

In Chapters 1 and 2, you created an essay map for each paper you wrote: a brief outline of the essay, including the thesis statement and the topic sentences for your essay's paragraphs. An essay map is an organizational tool that helps you visualize your entire essay. (Review the process for writing an essay map in Chapter 1, p. 25.) Because the map is a "work-in-progress," you may revise or even change your ideas as you focus and organize your essay.

The essay map for your persuasive essay should contain a thesis statement of opinion. That is, your thesis statement should do more than introduce the two qualities of effective learning that focus your essay. It tells your readers whether one or both of the characteristics contribute to successful learning in online courses.

Here are samples of effective thesis statements of opinion. Notice that your thesis statement may be (1) positive about both selected characteristics, (2) negative about both characteristics, or (3) positive about one characteristic but negative about the other.

positive opinion about both features

1. If both the instructor and the students are highly motivated, the features of <u>student-instructor discussion</u> and <u>collaborative student projects</u> contribute as much to learning in online courses as they do in a traditional classroom.

negative opinion about both features

2. Therefore, even though <u>collaboration on projects</u> and <u>group problem solving</u> can exist in both the classroom and as part of online courses, neither characteristic functions as well in e-courses.

positive opinion about the first feature and negative opinion about the second feature

3. Although <u>faculty-student communication</u> can contribute to successful learning in both the traditional classroom and in online courses, <u>the formation of a community of students</u> through use of a discussion board is often less successful for e-learners.

Following is an example of an essay map written for this chapter writing assignment. This essay map includes only the essay's working thesis statement of opinion and topic sentences.

Essay Map: Online Education and Learning Styles

Introductory Paragraph Thesis statement of opinion	Distance learners can access online course materials designed to accommodate diverse learning styles, and they can choose to demonstrate their learning in a variety of ways.
Background Paragraph Topic Sentence	Learning styles are crucial to success in college courses.
Body Paragraph 1 Topic Sentence	Students of all learning styles benefit from e-courses.
Body Paragraph 2 Topic Sentence	E-learning allows students to learn in different ways.
Concluding Paragraph	Students with varying needs can enjoy success in online learning.

EXERCISE 12 Creating your essay map

Construct an essay map for your persuasive essay that includes at least a working thesis statement of opinion and a topic sentence for each paragraph. You may also choose to include supporting information. Be sure to consider your readers (and what they may or may not know about your topic) as you construct your essay map.

SPOTLIGHT ON WRITING SKILLS

Background Paragraphs

In addition to reading articles about online education, you acquired supporting information about your topic through your interview of an expert. Readers expect to be told about the experts whose work you read, the expert(s) you spoke with in interviews, and the questions you asked during your interview(s). Often, this information is provided in the background paragraph.

Following is an example of how one student listed information she wanted to use in her background paragraph. The focus of her paragraph is a description of the processes she used to gather information for her paper: the Internet and library research she did and the interview information she collected.

Background Paragraph Information

1) Overall statement—researched two features of online learning:
   faculty-study interaction
   discussion boards

2) Researched on the Internet and in the library about my two qualities that contribute to online learning.

3) Interviewed one student who has taken online courses; asked him how faculty-student interaction and discussion boards contributed to his classroom and online learning.

4) Interviewed an instructor who has taught online courses. I also asked her for her opinions on faculty-student interaction and discussion boards and how they contribute to learning.

EXERCISE 13 Analyzing a paragraph

Read the following student paragraphs, and review the comments in the margin. Draw a line to connect each comment to the appropriate section in the paragraphs. Then, with a partner, answer the questions that follow.

Student Essay: Introductory and Background Paragraphs

Introductory paragraph begins with a statement that is generally accepted.

Results of interviews with students support the introductory claim.

The paragraph ends with a thesis statement of opinion (positive about both features evaluated in this paper).

The topic sentence of the background paragraph introduces the process followed in this study.

Online education presents many advantages for busy students who require flexibility in their schedules. Recent data collected in interviews with e-campus college students solidly supports this point. When asked "Why do you take classes online?," a great majority mentioned the convenience of having access to course materials 24 hours a day and being able to study whenever and wherever they want to. (See student interview results in Appendix B.) However, do distance students perform as well as their peers on campus when it comes to learning course material and passing tests? Some claim "yes," and others say "no." This difference of opinion is not surprising given the wide variety of learning preferences of college students, both online and on campus. However, with current technology and methodology, today distance learners can easily access online course materials that have been designed to accommodate diverse learning styles; similarly, they can choose to demonstrate their learning in a variety of effective ways.

To evaluate distance education today, the class read several articles by experts in the field and then designed sets of questions for online instructors and students to answer. (See Appendix A for interview questions; Appendix D for suggested readings.) Pairs of students then selected two features of online courses to study in depth and wrote further questions on these subjects. Each pair interviewed at least one e-campus instructor

An explanation of how information was gathered includes logical organizers (*then*, *when*) that show chronological order.

The background paragraph ends by briefly describing the results of the interviews.

and two or three students, in person and/or via e-mail. When the interviews were completed, the class compiled, categorized, and analyzed the overall perceptions of online learning that they had collected. Results showed that for the most part, students and faculty are happy with their online experiences. Many students described their e-courses as "challenging," but when discussing the presentation of course materials and online testing, most said that they enjoyed taking the responsibility for their own learning and assessment.

Reference

Ko, S., & Rossen, S. (2004). *Teaching online: A practical guide.* Boston: Houghton Mifflin.

1. Circle the strategy used by the writer to begin the introductory paragraph:

   a question   a provocative, interesting statement

   a quotation   a general, non-controversial statement

   a fact or statistic   a brief, interesting story

   a definition

2. Underline the thesis statement of opinion, and circle the controlling ideas.

3. Reread the thesis statement. What features of online learning environments will the writer evaluate?

   _____

   _____

   _____

   _____

4. How many body paragraphs do you expect to be developed in this essay? Why?

   _____

   _____

5. Write three questions you expect will be answered in the body
   paragraphs of this essay.

   _____

   _____

   _____

   _____

☐ **Drafting, Revising, and Editing**

EXERCISE **14** **Planning and drafting your paragraphs**

Plan and draft your paragraphs by completing these steps:

1. Reread the chapter writing assignment. Carefully consider your
   working thesis statement of opinion and topic sentences included
   in your essay map. Revise them if necessary.
2. Reread the information you included on the "introduction"
   information page you created in Exercise 11. Then, plan and draft
   an introductory paragraph that will (a) interest your readers,
   (b) provide brief information about your topic, and (c) include
   your thesis statement of opinion.
3. Reread the information you included on the "background"
   information page you created in Exercise 11. Then, plan and draft
   your background paragraph by considering the following questions:
   a. What information about online education do your readers need
      to know to understand the rest of the essay?
   b. What important words and phrases are associated with online
      courses? Should any of those key terms be defined for your readers?
   c. What historical and/or factual information about the development
      of electronic courses might help your readers relate to the topic of
      your essay?
   d. If you gathered information about your topic through an
      interview, explain this to your readers.

4. Include in-text citations for all sources (including your interview) referred to or included in the paragraphs. Example citations for interviews follow:

   In-text citation:
   One student who is taking two courses online stated that he sometimes has to wait twelve hours for a reply to his discussion board comments (D. Beckington, personal communication, November 12, 2004).

   End-of-text reference:
   There is no end-of-text reference. Because your readers cannot retrieve the data you gathered from an interview, your interview source information is not included in your end-of-text reference page.

5. Begin to draft a reference page that includes source information (but not "personal communications" information).

EXERCISE 15 Revising your paragraphs

Before you ask a classmate for feedback, review and revise your writing.

1. Read your paragraphs carefully, and consider these questions:
   a. Does your thesis statement include your opinion and the reason(s) for your opinion?
   b. Does your background paragraph begin with a topic sentence that has controlling ideas?
   c. Have you adequately provided factual and/or historical information about your topic and/or explained how you gathered your information?
   d. Have you defined key terms?
   e. Have you included in-text citations when you used outside sources?
   f. Have you used a variety of attribution signals with your paraphrases or quotes?
   g. Does your reference page include all outside sources referred to or included in your paragraphs?
2. Make any changes that improve the meaning of your writing.
3. Save your revisions in a word-processed document, and print one copy.

EXERCISE 16 **Providing and receiving peer feedback**

Provide and receive feedback by completing the following:

1. Exchange papers with a partner, and read your partner's paragraphs. Do not hold a pen or pencil in your hand during this first reading. Read for the overall meaning first.

2. Read the paragraphs again. This time, complete the following:
   a. In the margin, write the technique that was used in the introduction to engage the reader:

question	provocative, interesting statement
quotation	general, non-controversial statement
fact or statistic	brief, interesting story
definition	

   b. Do you think the thesis statement of opinion is clear? That is, does it (1) present the two characteristics of effective learning and (2) give an opinion about the value of each feature in an online learning environment? Underline the two characteristics, and circle the opinion(s) in the thesis statement.
   c. In the margins, write the types of supporting information (e.g., historical information, key term and definition, method of research) provided in the background paragraph.
   d. Place a plus sign (+) in the margin of the background paragraph next to the supporting detail you find most helpful for the readers. Be ready to explain why to your partner.
   e. Put brackets [ ] around each in-text citation. Is each a correct APA citation? If not, suggest a correction in the margin.
   f. Check the reference page to make sure that all outside sources are included and listed correctly. If not, suggest corrections in the margins of the page.

3. Return your partner's paper, and reread your own introductory and background paragraphs. Notice the marks and comments your partner made. Ask your partner any questions you have for clarification.

4. Consider what you learned about academic writing from reviewing your partner's paragraphs.

5. Mark and make notes about revisions you want to make to your writing. These marks and comments will be your "revision plan."

EXERCISE 17 **Revising and editing your paragraphs**

Reread your introductory and background paragraphs and your reference page. Consider your revision plan as you begin revising your paragraphs. Make at least two changes that improve your writing. Edit for grammar, punctuation, and spelling to reflect your best work. Save your revisions in a word-processed document. Your instructor may also want to collect your paragraphs for review or evaluation.

SPOTLIGHT ON WRITING SKILLS

Avoiding Plagiarism

As you begin to write your essay, you want to eliminate any possibility of *plagiarizing*. Plagiarism is a form of cheating. You plagiarize if you use the words, ideas, or art of others without giving the original author credit. Here are some examples of plagiarism:

a. A student copies the written words of another author but does not credit the author with an in-text citation and an end-of-text reference.

b. A student copies most of the words of another author but changes the sentence structure and adds some words such as *and*, *so*, or *this* but does not credit the author with an in-text citation and an end-of-text reference.

c. A student copies the ideas, but not the exact words, of another author but does not credit the author with an in-text citation and an end-of-text reference.

d. A student summarizes the ideas of another author but does not credit the author with an in-text citation and an end-of-text reference.

Whether intentional or not, plagiarism is a serious academic offense. A student found plagiarizing can be given an automatic failing grade in the course; that student may also be subject to expulsion or suspension from school.

Fortunately, plagiarism is easy to avoid. The rules are simple:

Rule 1:   Any information you did not know about your topic before you began to gather information about it must be cited (with in-text citation and end-of-text reference).

Rule 2:   If you copy more than three contiguous words (words that occur together) from a source, use quotation marks around the copied material and cite that material (with in-text citation and end-of-text reference).

Sometimes students believe that they should quote directly from the writing of others because the published writers are more experienced. However, college instructors expect students to paraphrase or summarize most materials. Students should rarely use direct quotations in their papers and should use long quotations (more than 40 words) even more rarely. This chapter discusses summary writing so that you can gain confidence and competence with this important skill. Paraphrasing skills are discussed in Chapter 2, page 81. Review and practice them often.

EXERCISE 18   **Understanding degrees of plagiarism**

With a small group of classmates, discuss whether each of the following scenarios constitutes plagiarism. Then, compare your opinions with your classmates'.

1. While researching a topic on the Internet, you come across a great five-paragraph essay. You read the entire essay for ideas but copy only the thesis statement for your own essay.
2. You want to quote a paragraph from a textbook, but you know it is too long. Instead, you put quotation marks around the first two lines when you use the text in your essay, and follow that with the author's name in parentheses. Then, you simply paraphrase the rest of the original paragraph in your own words.
3. You are taking the same psychology class that your friend took last semester. You have a different instructor, but the assignments are identical. Your friend gives you all her notes and papers to study. You revise one of her papers and turn it in to your instructor for a grade.

4. You cannot find enough information to complete the outline for your research paper in your U.S. history class. You ask your former English instructor for help. She looks through your textbook with you, offers feedback on what you have done, and helps you construct a solid thesis statement and full-sentence outline for a 1,000-word essay.

5. While researching the life of a prominent politician, you come across some commonly known facts, such as where he is from, what offices he has held, and how he is likely to vote on controversial issues. Although you include much of this information in your introductory and background paragraphs, you do not document the source of this information.

6. While searching the Internet, you discover a website that provides sample essays about your topic. You download three of those samples and include two to four sentences from one essay in your paper. You do not list the essays in your reference page.

WEB POWER

For more information about avoiding plagiarism and using proper citation, visit the website for this book at **http://esl.college.hmco.com/students.**

SPOTLIGHT ON WRITING SKILLS

Summarizing

Usually, the information from sources that you use in your background and body paragraphs are summarized: A *summary* is a brief restatement of the main idea(s) of a longer piece of writing. Summarizing is an essential academic skill. You often summarize instructors' lectures, as well as material you read. For instance, in the answer to an examination question, you might summarize information from your reading or class notes.

In your academic essays, you will frequently summarize information you find on the Internet or in books or journals. The main goal of academic summary writing is to provide readers with a brief, clear report of main ideas in written material that the readers may not have read.

Here are some conventions of summary writing:

1. Summaries are often only one-half or one-quarter as long as the original material. For lengthy works (such as books), they may be even shorter.
2. Each summary has a beginning, a middle, and an end. In that way, the summary reflects the beginning, middle, and end of the original material.
3. A summary usually begins by mentioning the author(s) and/or title of the original material and the key point of the original source.
4. Summary writers paraphrase the words used in the original material.
5. Usually the keywords in the original material remain the same in the summary.
6. Combining more than one main idea from the original material into a single sentence helps reduce overall word count and repetition in a summary.

Following are steps to follow when summarizing:

a. Carefully read to understand the original source. Use a dictionary or ask your instructor to clarify terms or concepts you cannot understand in context.
b. Identify the main ideas and essential supporting details.
c. On separate paper, take notes of the important ideas. Do not copy complete sentences.
d. Use only your notes as you begin to write your summary.
e. At the beginning of your summary, state the source and the main idea of the entire passage.
f. Include all main idea(s) in your summary (usually in the order they were originally presented).
g. Include only the supporting details that are necessary to understanding the main points.
h. Omit personal opinions.
i. Use cohesion devices (like logical organizers) to help your summary read smoothly. See Appendix 3, "Logical Organizers," for a list of logical organizers.

EXERCISE 19 Analyzing a summary

Following is an original text and a summary of that text. As you read both, review summary conventions by reading the comments in the margin. Then, with a partner, complete the questions that follow.

Original Text

The text begins with a topic sentence.

"Our" indicates that this text is a paragraph from an article reporting the authors' research.

Quotation marks are not used because this paragraph is the original text.

One characteristic of effective learning is the area of discussion among classmates. Such interaction is potentially an ideal place for students to form a learning community, but instructors should not assume that all students will participate or learn from this form of collaboration, particularly in online courses. Our recent research demonstrated that student progress in economics classes result in better performance by classroom students than by online students. The research indicates that the differences were due to access to the instructor and to cooperation with fellow students in classroom courses, facets that are unavailable to online students.

Source: Chizmar, J.F., & Walbert, M.S. (1999). Web-based learning environment guided by principles of good teaching practice. *Journal of Economic Education, 30*, 3, 248–250. Retrieved November 11, 2004, from http://www.indiana.edu/~econed/ pdffiles/Summer99/chizmar.pdf.

Summary

The summary begins by stating the authors and main idea of the article.

Only main ideas and essential supporting details are included.

Research by Chizmar and Walbert (1999) showed that students in classroom-based economics courses achieved more than online students in the same course. The research revealed that e-students had less interaction with the instructor and fewer opportunities to collaborate with classmates.

1. Count the number of words in each paragraph: original source

   _____ , summary _____. How much briefer is the

   summary? _____

2. Circle the main ideas and important details in the original text. Draw
   lines to connect them to the ideas in the summary. If the ideas are not

included in the summary, write a question mark (?) next to the ideas in the original text.

3. Are any main ideas in the original materials missing from the summary? Explain your opinion.

_____

_____

4. Are any important supporting details missing from the summary? Explain your opinion.

_____

_____

5. How does the summary fulfill (or not fulfill) the conventions of summary writing listed previously?

_____

_____

_____

POWER GRAMMAR

Using the Grammar and Punctuation of Summary Writing

Use certain grammar and punctuation structures when you write effective summaries. The following illustrates some of those structures.

1. Chiraz (2005) *described* the necessity of using the discussion board at least once a week. In the conclusion of the report, Gray (2004) *predicted* that online instructors will add advances in technology to their courses.	Use reporting verbs (or other attribution signals) and past tense verbs. (See Appendix 2 for more information.)

The results of Johnson's research *indicate* that one major draw-back of online discussion boards is their asynchronicity (2005).	However, use present tense reporting verbs when presenting research results or when reporting "general truth."
2. Instead of <u></u> Use<u></u> achieved succeeded collaborate cooperate e-students online students	Use synonyms for words when possible.
3. Time: *first, second, then* Cause: *because, as, since* Emphasis: *in fact, indeed* Example: *for instance, as an illustration*	Use logical organizers to help readers move from one idea to the next. Some categories and example logical organizers are provided. See Appendix 4, "Logical Organizers," for a more extensive list.
4. In Wyman's article "The Power of Your Personal Learning Style," the author states that . . . (2003). The research of online instructor Glenn Merrick (2005) is reported in his book, *Teaching, Learning, and Technology.* *Seven Principles for Good Practice in Undergraduate Education* *The Online Future*	Within your essay, use correct capitalization and punctuation for titles of original materials: ▪ The titles of journal, Internet, or newspaper articles written in an essay are put in quotation marks, and all major words are capitalized. ▪ The titles of books and newspapers written in an essay are italicized or underlined, and all major words are capitalized. ▪ Prepositions (*with, by*), articles (*an, the*), and conjunctions (*and, but*) are not capitalized unless they appear as the first word of the title.

5. End-of-Text Reference: Wyman, P. (2003, June 6). The power of your personal learning style. *How to learn*. Retrieved April 29, 2004, from http://www.howto learn.com/personal.html	Use correct APA in-text citations and end-of-text references. ■ See APA in-text citations in the previous examples. Also see Appendix 1, "In-text Citation: APA Style of Documentation." ■ Notice the differences between capitalization of titles written in the essay and on the reference page. For more information about end-of-text references, see Appendix 3, "End-of-Text References: APA Style of Documentation." ■ Notice how end-of-text references are indented and double-spaced.

EXERCISE 20 Practicing summary writing

Practice summary writing by completing the following:

1. Write a summary for each of these paragraphs which are about 100 words long. Follow the conventions for summary writing and the grammar and punctuation for summary writing discussed previously.

Paragraph 1

"Because electronic communication is readily available, the chance for students to work with others has been greatly extended. Not only can faculty expect students to find classmates who can share ideas about a project, they can also contact scholars throughout the world. It is possible to visit sites or join groups where advanced scholars share ideas. A student could be expected to post his or her thoughts to one of these individuals or groups and receive advice, support, and suggestions from colleagues. It is not uncommon to encounter requests from graduate students beginning a project, collecting information, or asking for feedback. Connected to projects like this, electronic communication becomes a powerful way to attempt projects that are subject to complex responses."

Source: O'Connor, T. (2004). *Using learning styles to adapt technology for higher education.* Indiana State University Center for Teaching and Learning. Retrieved on April 15, 2004, from http://web.indstate.edu/ctl/styles/learning.html

Paragraph 2

"A method appropriate for most students may be ineffective for other students who could learn more easily with a different approach. Methods of teaching (e.g., graphic or verbal), ways of representing information and personality characteristics of teachers all affect learning and affect different learners differently. Thinking about learning styles can lead a teacher to think about different ways of teaching, and that is good. An effective teacher needs to vary techniques and to have a variety of teaching methods and learning activities to draw upon from moment to moment or from week to week to facilitate maximum learning for as many students as possible."

Source: McKeachie, W.J. (1995, November). Learning styles can become learning strategies. *The National Teaching and Learning Forum, Volume 4, Number 6.* Retrieved April 18, 2004, from http://www.ntlf.com/html/pi/9511/article1.htm

2. Exchange your summaries with a classmate, and complete the following:
   a. Underline the main ideas and essential supporting details in each original paragraph, and identify them in the summaries. If you cannot locate a main idea or essential supporting detail in the summary, place an asterisk (*) next to the idea in the original text.
   b. Look back at the original texts if you disagree with the accuracy of your classmate's summaries, and write a question mark (?) next to your concerns in the margin of the summary.
   c. Compare the length of your partner's summaries to the original texts. Are the summaries much shorter than the original texts (no more than half the length)? If not, write a note about the length in the margin.

      d. At the bottom of each summary, write one aspect you think was effective and write one suggestion to improve your partner's writing.

  3. Return your partner's paper.

      a. Reread your own summaries. Notice the marks and comments made by your partner. Ask your partner any questions you have for clarification.

      b. Discuss the summarizing strategies you used to write your summaries.

- What summarizing conventions or steps did you follow?
- What grammar and punctuation techniques did you use?
- What problems did you have summarizing the ideas?
- What did you learn about summarizing from practicing these techniques?

EXERCISE 21 Analyzing a persuasive essay

Read the following student essay, and study the comments provided in the margin. Draw lines to connect the comments to the appropriate section of the paragraphs. Then, with a classmate, answer the questions that follow.

Student Essay: Features of Online Learning

The introductory paragraph begins with a statement that is generally accepted.

Brief comments about the topic are included.

The paragraph ends with a thesis statement of opinion (acknowledgment of negative opinion, but focus on positive opinions of discussion boards).

    A good learning environment includes many important characteristics, and a good instructor knows how to design and teach classes that incorporate these features. Two essential components of college courses outlined in a national study by Chickering and Gamson (1987) are the opportunity for students to engage in collaborative learning with their classmates and the necessity for prompt and effective feedback from their instructors. Early proponents of online learning saw great potential in both of these areas, claiming first that the discussion board, or online forum, would offer students the ideal opportunity to collaborate from a distance and that communication via e-mail would provide students with quick, helpful feedback from instructors (Chickering & Erhmann, 1996). More recently, numerous interviews with online students and faculty at St. Petersburg College have suggested that, by and large, these positive predictions of online learning have proved correct. Although improvements to the discussion area were recommended for distance students to create a better sense of community and learn collaboratively with their peers, student-instructor interaction in online courses is frequent, effective, and highly motivating for online students.

In the fall of 2004, personal interviews with online students and faculty members at St. Petersburg College revealed that e-courses had become a highly valued addition to traditional courses taught on campus. In fact, 39 of the 47 students interviewed stated that they would definitely take more courses via the Internet. (See results of student interviews in Appendix B.) An impressive 90 percent of the instructors surveyed (17 of 19) reported that they planned to continue teaching at least one distance course per semester. (See results of faculty interviews in Appendix C.) Interviewees were asked to rate and explain their views on several features of online learning such as multimedia presentations, interactive tests, online discussion areas, and technological support. In addition to considering overall findings, each research team compiled and analyzed ratings and responses that focused on key features of learning that they had selected to study and evaluate. In terms of developing a sense of community with peers through online discussions and interacting regularly with instructors in discussions and e-mail, students and instructors seemed to agree that collaborative learning online may not have reached its potential but that student-instructor contact plays an integral part in making online courses enjoyable and effective.

To begin with, use of the discussion board to facilitate collaboration among students received mixed ratings. Students who were dissatisfied with online discussions provided valid reasons that must be considered. According to many, the major drawback of "discussing" topics online is that the communication is asynchronous, meaning that class participants are not on task at the same time. One student who is taking two courses online stated that he sometimes has to wait twelve hours for a single reply from a fellow student, and by then, he has usually either lost interest in the topic or does not have time to deal with it (D. Beck, personal communication, October 14, 2004). Another student who has completed several e-courses called these online interactions "tedious" and "dreary." He stated, as did several of the students surveyed, that students usually respond to what classmates write because they are required to do so, not because

---

The topic sentence of the background paragraph includes the topic (interaction component of e-courses) and controlling idea (valued form of education).

Explanation of how information was gathered is given.

Interview results are provided.

The topic is narrowed to one main feature (discussion boards—focus on less positive views).

A term related to the topic (*asynchronous*) is defined.

The experts (interviewees) are identified as credible sources.

In-text citations for the interviews is included.

they want to (N. Nazemi, personal communication, October 11, 2004). One interviewee suggested that college students today are used to exchanging ideas in real-time with instant messaging, chatrooms, and Web cameras, and therefore would be more likely to participate in discussions if synchronous and/or audio communication became a regular part of their online course work (T. Kim, personal communication, November 5, 2004). One obvious solution to encourage more collaboration among students, then, is for online instructors to use advanced technologies that their students are already accustomed to.

The paragraph ends with a possible solution.

The topic sentence indicates that positive views will be discussed.

The interviewee is identified as a credible source.

Still, not all students expressed negative views about the discussion boards in their e-courses, and most faculty reported that the online forums in their courses were lively and productive. Professor Kevin Morgan, who has been a pioneer in online learning since 1998 and holds an Ed.D. in Instructional Technology and Distance Education, described online discussions as one of the great strengths of his courses. He pointed out that many students need time to reflect and construct responses; they often do not take part in face-to-face discussions on campus but enjoy the "safe and anonymous environment" of interacting online (K. Morgan, personal communication, October 26, 2004). Nonnative speakers of English, for instance, may feel more comfortable discussing college material with their American peers online rather than in person. One Japanese student who was interviewed said she first writes her entries for the discussion area in a word processing program so that she can check her spelling and grammar before posting her writing for everyone to read. Although this takes time, she contributes more than she would in a live discussion, she said. She added that her English is becoming better with all this writing practice (M. Nakamura, personal communication, October 18, 2004). Another student, a sophomore who has taken several courses online, favors the "low technology requirements of the discussion board and access 24/7" because these features allow all students to participate and share their personalities online (J. Ortamendi, personal communication, October 29, 2004). Dr. Morgan agreed. In his experience, he has seen that "[students] form collaborative bonds witnessed in their heartfelt goodbyes at the close of each semester" (K. Morgan, personal communication, October 26, 2004).

Support for the expert's comments is provided (another student comment).

A direct quote is included, and a word added to the quote is placed in brackets [ ].

Topic sentence indicates focus is on the success of online learning.

Support for that claim is offered.

A direct quote from a student is included.

Readers are directed to the essay's appendix, where they can find interview questions.

     While the ability to form a sense of community and promote collaborative learning online seems to be a matter of personal experience and opinion, the use of e-mail to foster communication between students and their instructors is generally accepted as a great success. Several students commented that they "speak" to their online instructors much more than they do with instructors on campus because they usually have little time between classes or their instructors' office hours do not match their own schedules. With e-mail, no appointment time is necessary. One student taking her first online course this semester was surprised at the fast, detailed responses her instructor sent, many times within minutes or hours. She was not sure if all e-campus instructors responded to e-mail this quickly, but she said, "I will definitely take another course with this teacher!" (B. Patel, personal communication, October 22, 2004). In fact, the data collected showed that over 70 percent of instructors responded to student e-mail within 24 hours, including weekends. When asked what course tool was most important to running a successful online class, 88 percent of instructors responded "e-mail" (See results of faculty interviews in Appendix C.) Steven Gilbert, the president of the Teaching, Learning, and Technology Group, makes a further point about the effectiveness of electronic communication in his informative and convincing article titled "Why Bother?" Gilbert discusses research that has shown "a rise in course-related communication between students and faculty AFTER the completion of a course" (Gilbert, 2001, para. 19). This suggests that students who have had many question-and-answer sessions via e-mail throughout a course are motivated to learn more about the subject—not for a grade, but for enrichment. That should be the goal of any teaching and learning environment.

A logical organizer (*to conclude*) signals the conclusion to the essay.

Main ideas of the essay are briefly restated.

To conclude, the class discussion area is potentially an ideal place for distance students to form an effective learning community, but instructors should not assume that all students will participate in or learn from this form of collaboration in similar ways. Adding alternatives, such as synchronous chat areas and video messages with webcams, may increase participation and enhance learning for diverse groups of online students. E-mail serves as an excellent tool for instructor-student interaction. This frequent contact can motivate students to achieve high standards and stimulate instructors to offer thoughtful feedback. By taking advantage of existing technology and keeping abreast of new options as they become available, distance educators and students will continue to engage in effective learning environments that may eventually surpass those of traditional classrooms.

A prediction is offered at the end of the concluding paragraph.

Because readers cannot retrieve the data you gathered from an interview, your interview source information is not included in your reference list.

References

Chickering, A., & Ehrmann, S. (1996). Implementing the seven principles: Technology as lever. *AAHE Bulletin*, October, pp. 3–6. Retrieved November 6, 2004, from http://www.tltgroup.org/programs/seven.html

Chickering, A., & Gamson, Z. (1987). Seven principles for good practices in undergraduate education. *AAHE Bulletin*. Retrieved October 28, 2004, from http://www.hcc.hawaii.edu/intranet/communities/FacDevCom/guidebk/teachtip/7princip.htm

1. Underline the thesis statement.

2. In the margins of the essay, identify the paragraphs (e.g., introduction, background). How many body paragraphs are there? How do the body paragraphs connect to the thesis statement?

   _____

   _____

   _____

   _____

3. Locate two or three quotations in the essay, and discuss the use of punctuation and in-text citation.

   _____

   _____

   _____

   _____

4. What concluding strategy (e.g., call for action, suggestion) did the writer use for this essay? What other strategy could have been used?

   _____

   _____

   _____

   _____

P O W E R   G R A M M A R

Using Language to Control the Strength of an Opinion

In persuasive essays, you want to convince your readers to believe your claims or opinions. Effective writers use certain language structures to control the strength and validity of their claims.

---

1. *Most* students agreed that the major drawback of the online discussion board is that it is asynchronous. One student stated, as did *the majority of* the students interviewed, that they *usually* respond to what classmates write because they are required to do so, not because they want to. One solution *seems to be* that online instructors *should* investigate the use of these more advanced technologies.	**Valid Claims** In these sentences, the italicized words limit the strength of the claim, making the claim more valid or believable. For example, in the first sentence, "most" students agree, but not "all."

When claims are too strong, readers may consider your opinions inaccurate or invalid and may not be persuaded to agree with you.

2. *Students* agreed that the major draw-back of the online discussion board is that it is asynchronous.	**Invalid Claims** In these sentences, the writer's claims may be inaccurate or too strong. Some readers may disagree with the claims.

One student stated, as did the students interviewed, that *they respond* to what classmates write because they are required to do so, not because they want to.	For example, this sentence implies that "all" the students interviewed (not the "majority") responded in the same way.
Online instructors *must investigate* the use of these more advanced technologies.	In the last sentence, the modal "must" may be too strong.

Various language structures control the strength of a generalization. This chart illustrates some of those structures.

3. Different students bring different talents and styles to college. Brilliant students in a seminar *might be* all thumbs in a lab; students rich in hands-on experience *may not do* so well with theory.	<u>Modal auxiliaries</u> *may, might, could, ought to* (instead of *must* or *will* or no modal auxiliary)
4. The range of technologies that encourage active learning is staggering. *Many* fall into one of three categories: tools and resources for learning by doing, time-delayed exchange, and real-time conversation.	<u>Expressions of quantity</u> *a number of, many, some, few* (instead of *all* or *none*)

5. It *tends* to be easier to discuss values and personal concerns in writing than orally, because inadvertent or ambiguous nonverbal signals are not so dominant.	Certain verbs *seem to, appear to, tend to, suggest, indicate*
6. Working with others *often* increases involvement in learning.	Adverbs of frequency *frequently, often, usually, rarely* (instead of *always* or *never*)
7. Faculty report that students *generally* feel stimulated by knowing their finished work will be "published" on the World Wide Web.	Other adverbs and adjectives *perhaps, largely, essentially, generally, basically, mainly*
8. Total communication between students and faculty increases via e-mail and the WWW, and *for the most part*, the results seem more intimate and convenient than face-to-face communication.	Certain phrases *by and large, for the most part, in part*

Source: Chickering, A.W., & Ehrmann, S.C. (1996). Implementing the seven principles: Technology as lever. *AAHE Bulletin.* Retrieved May 17, 2004, from http://www.tltgroup.org/programs/seven.html

EXERCISE 22   Using language to control opinions

Complete the following steps:

1. Read the following comments offered by instructors and students familiar with online courses. Underline examples of language that control the strength of opinions. One example from the first paragraph is underlined as an example.

   a. E-mail is an effective way to communicate with my instructor. I <u>often</u> contact my instructor to set up appointments or ask questions through e-mail. Sometimes, my instructor asks us to e-mail our assignments instead of turning in a paper copy. We can also submit assignments from home when we are unable to attend class.

   b. Electronic communication seems to be a nonthreatening way for instructors and students to communicate with each other. For the most part, my students seem uncomfortable meeting during my office hours. With e-mail and discussion boards, however, they can communicate whenever it is convenient for them. In fact, I believe that my students' satisfaction with my course is largely due to the ability to easily contact me or their classmates when they have questions about the course.

2. Weaken the tone of the following arguments by adding three or four language structures in each paragraph. One example is provided in the first paragraph.

   Perhaps

   a. ₍ₐ₎The biggest advantage of electronic communication is that it increases interaction between me and my instructors. In the past, I asked questions and made comments only in the classroom and during my instructors' office hours. However, e-mail and discussion boards have changed all that. My communication and interaction with my instructors has greatly increased.

b. Instructors complain about the use of electronic communication with their students. They report that they receive too many e-mails from students, making it time-consuming to respond to this communication. In addition, students expect immediate responses from their e-mails, and this is not possible for instructors with faculty commitments outside the classroom.

EXERCISE 23 **Planning and drafting your body paragraphs**

The chapter writing assignment states that your persuasive essay should include two or three body paragraphs that describe and explain your chosen features of online learning. You should also provide your opinion about the contributions of those qualities in an online learning environment and support your opinions with facts, expert opinions, experiences, and examples.

1. To help you draft your body paragraphs, review your essay map. For each body paragraph, follow the conventions of academic writing that you have practiced so far in this course:
   - Write a topic sentence with a clear main idea and controlling idea(s).
   - Provide clear, convincing explanations and examples to persuade your readers.
   - Summarize and paraphrase ideas as supporting points in your paper.
   - Introduce supporting points with clear, logical organizers.
   - Include cohesion devices to help your readers understand the connection of ideas.
   - Use appropriate structures that control the strength of opinions. Try to use structures you may not have used before, like by and large or for the most part.
   - Include appropriate in-text citation, and use a variety of attribution signals.
   - Provide information to explain the credibility of your outside sources.
   - Conclude with a statement that highlights your point of view.
2. Add all outside source information to your reference page.
3. Add and save your body paragraphs to your word-processed document. Your instructor may also want to collect a copy of your writing for review or evaluation.

EXERCISE 24 Planning and drafting your paragraph

To plan and draft your concluding paragraph, complete these steps:

1. Reread your entire essay to prepare to write the conclusion.
2. Reread your introductory paragraph, and decide how to relate to the main ideas in your introduction.
3. Identify and summarize one or two main ideas from the body paragraphs that you want to refer to in the conclusion. Use these ideas to refresh your readers' memory of the main points.
4. Decide what strategy to use at the end of your concluding paragraph (e.g., add a prediction, recommendation, solution).
5. Draft the concluding paragraph for your essay, and add the conclusion to your word-processed document.

 EXERCISE 25 Revising your persuasive essay

To revise your essay, complete these steps:

Master Student Tip

You will benefit from putting away the first draft of your completed essay for at least 24 hours. When you pick it up again, you will begin the revision process with a clear mind and the energy to work well.

1. To make sure you adequately fulfilled the assignment's requirements, review the chapter writing assignment again. Then, slowly and thoughtfully reread your entire essay. Make revisions where appropriate.
2. Review your reference page to be sure all sources you used when writing your paper are included. Use the form of the reference page shown in Appendix 3, "End-of-Text References: APA Style of Documentation."
3. Save and print a copy of your essay.

EXERCISE 26 Providing and receiving peer feedback

Work with a partner to complete the following:

1. Share copies of each other's essay. Read your partner's paper silently while your partner reads her or his essay aloud. Ask your partner questions to clarify main ideas and supporting details you find difficult to understand.
2. Then, read your partner's essay on your own. To offer feedback to your partner, refer to the feedback form located at http://esl.college.hmco.com/students.
3. Return and discuss each other's papers.

EXERCISE 27 **Finalizing your essay**

Complete these steps:

1. Consider your partner's suggestions and your own insights as you revise your essay.
2. Edit for and correct any errors in grammar, spelling, and punctuation.
3. Save the document as your final draft, and print one copy.
4. Attach your draft(s), your list of interview questions as an "appendix," and copies of all outside sources referred to while writing your paper. Submit your paper and attachments for your instructor's review and evaluation.

☐ More Practice and Self-Assessment

1. Write a paragraph advising a new group of students on the best ways to gather information, select and organize material, and write the persuasive essay for this chapter.
2. Complete a reference page for the following four sources.

Author(s):	Peri Waddell
Title of source:	The Advantages of Studying Online
Source type:	article in journal
Published in:	*TESOL Journal*
Date Published:	Summer 2004
Pages Cited:	18–21
Volume:	Vol. 5, No. 4

Author(s):	Sera Luedtke
Title of source:	Still Going Strong: Online Learning
Source type:	online newspaper article
Published in:	*Atlanta Journal-Constitution*
Date Published:	January 10, 2005
Pages Cited:	C22
Retrieved:	http://www.accessatlanta.com/ ajc/eday/news_c3g

Author(s):   none provided
Title of source: *UCLA TATP Teaching Tips: Managing Electronic Communication Tools*
Source type: website
Published in: online publication
Date Published: none provided
Pages Cited: entire source
Retrieved: http://www.oid.ucla. edu/Tatp/downloads/communication.pdf

Author(s):   Cathy L. Wald, Judy Gondreau, Sharla L. Klingaman
Title of source: *Online Education: A Wave of the Future?*
Source type: book
Published in: Boston: Intercultural Press
Date Published: February 2004
Pages Cited: 22–24

WEB POWER

You can find additional exercises related to the content in this chapter at **http://esl.college.hmco.com/students.**

Writing an Objective Report

Many college assignments require you to explore and investigate a topic. You might be asked to examine an issue you are studying in class or to investigate possible solutions to a problem or question. When you explore a topic, you may consult a variety of sources, like the Internet, a library, and people familiar with the topic.

Chapter Objectives

Read the following chapter objectives to preview the chapter content. After you complete the chapter, return to this chart and check (✓) the appropriate boxes on the right.	I have learned this well.	I need to work on this.
Follow a three-step writing process to gather, organize, and draft information		
Gather information from newspapers		
Complete Internet research		
Complete library research		
Practice active reading strategies		
Identify effective writing topics		
Write interview questions		
Use interview information in academic writing		
Organize ideas and details on "information" pages		
Understand expository essay development		
Create an essay map to further organize information		
Use a variety of sentences and style in academic writing		
Cite sources (in-text and end-of-text references)		

Chapter Writing Assignment

In this chapter, you will research and report on a controversy—a significant issue causing conflict in your local community. In an expository report of three to four pages, you will explain and discuss the two opposing sides of the issue. For this report, you will not propose a solution to the problem or agree with the position of one side over another. The purpose of this report is to inform your readers of the local controversy by summarizing, paraphrasing, and quoting from outside sources.

This assignment will require you to complete Internet and library searches and to interview people familiar with the issue and its controversy. It will require you to summarize and report on the information you have gathered.

Your report must include the following:

- An introductory paragraph
- A background paragraph that includes factual and/or historical information about your local issue
- Two to four body paragraphs that explain the issue and its two opposing sides
- A concluding paragraph
- At least two to four in-text citations
- An end-of-text reference page with references for all sources referred to as you wrote your paper

To complete your expository report, you will employ the three-step writing process:

1. Gathering Information
2. Focusing and Organizing
3. Drafting, Revising, and Editing

☐ Gathering Information

EXERCISE 1   **Understanding a controversial issue**

Read the following background information about a controversial issue and a news report about the same topic. Study the comments in the margin of the article. Then, with a classmate, answer the questions that follow.

Background Information

A controversial issue has occurred in Florida over a government decision outlining plans to clean up the Everglades in an effort to restore this national treasure to its natural state. The decision prompted negative reactions and criticism from businesses, interest groups, and concerned citizens. All the groups disapprove of the government's plan but for different reasons. They disagree on issues such as methods of measuring chemicals in water and what proportions of these chemicals make water harmful to humans, animals, and plants.

Sugar cane farmers in South Florida, for example, use fertilizers for a good crop each year, but the runoff from their irrigation systems contains phosphate, a mineral with many commercial uses such as for fertilizer. Phosphate harms native plants in the Everglades and makes unwanted plants grow more quickly. Of course, sugar farmers do not want to upset the natural environment of the Everglades. However, they fear that strict government rules concerning how much phosphate will be allowed will damage their sugar industry.

In contrast, the Miccosukee Indians who live in the Everglades area have a different point of view. They want chemicals banned from the Everglades and the land returned to a natural state with clean water flowing through the area. Many environmentalist groups such as the Audubon Society and Sierra Club agree. They want the Florida Department of Environmental Protection and other government agencies to work more diligently on the clean-up effort in the Everglades.

Professional Writing Sample: Newspaper Article

The topic sentence introduces the controversy.

The opening sentences provide background info: who, what, when, where.

Specific action taken by opposing groups is described.

Headline: Everglades Pollution Plan Draws Criticism

West Palm Beach – An Everglades pollution limit that Governor Jeb Bush's administration touts as one of its top environmental accomplishments took hits Thursday from all sides.

Five environmental groups and the Miccosukee Indian tribe filed legal challenges denouncing the limit as too lenient, and two subsidiaries of the sugar company, Florida Crystals Corp., attacked it as too strict.

Both sets of critics filed challenges with the state Division of Administrative Hearings on Thursday. That was the legal deadline for opposing the pollution rule that the state Environmental Regulation Commission approved July 8.

Newspaper articles do not always follow the conventions of academic writing (e.g., sentences in newspapers might begin with a coordinator like *but* and *and*).

On your reference page, capitalize titles carefully—notice the capitalization used in the article title and the newspaper title. Also, notice that the newspaper title is italicized.

The rule sets a limit of 10 parts per billion for phosphorus, a fertilizing chemical that scientists blame for fueling a growth of noxious cattails and upending the food chain in parts of the Everglades.

But the rule also spells out complicated methods for measuring the pollution and enforcing the limit. And those details went beyond what state law allows, the critics argue.

Reference

King, R. (2003, August 8). Everglades pollution plan draws criticism. *The Palm Beach Post*. Retrieved September 10, 2003, from http://www.nrdc.org/newsDetails.asp?nID=1053

1. What is the central issue causing controversy?

   _____

   _____

2. Who are the two opposing groups?

   _____

   _____

3. What viewpoint does each group have about the controversy?

   _____

   _____

   _____

4. Which paragraph in the news report explains the major reason for the criticism?

   _____

   _____

5. Whose opinions does the reporter cite? How do you know?

   _____

   _____

   _____

SPOTLIGHT ON WRITING SKILLS

Controversial Issues

In Chapter 3, you formed an opinion and supported that opinion with facts, research results, and ideas from experts to persuade your readers to share the same conclusion as you. In this chapter's writing assignment, however, you will not form an opinion. Instead, you will present both sides of an issue causing conflict in your community to educate your readers about the controversy. A controversial issue is similar to an opinion in that some people will agree with the topic and others will disagree. For example, some people would respond *yes* and others would respond *no* to this controversial question: *Should police mount surveillance cameras on city streets?*

Following are some controversial issues being discussed across the United States. Notice that each topic is written as a "should" question that can be answered either *yes* or *no*.

Controversy	Location
Should Little Beach continue to be a nude beach?	Maui, Hawaii
Should the school board fire the district superintendent?	Fort Collins, Colorado
Should the city spray pesticides in town to kill mosquitoes?	Laramie, Wyoming
Should the new flow plan for the Missouri River be passed?	Pierre, South Dakota
Should local officials grant building permits for a $500 million casino and resort area in the Catskill Mountains?	Thompson, New York
Should club owners pay for increased police power in the Buckhead club district?	Atlanta, Georgia

EXERCISE 2 **Writing about a controversial issue**

With your instructor and classmates, complete the following activities:

1. Make a list of controversial issues currently being discussed on your campus or in your community. Controversies may include decisions that must be made by the local government, conflicts that exist between groups of citizens or students, and proposals that are causing emotional reactions in your community.

2. Select two to three issues, and form a "should" question for each issue. Remember, an effective controversy, or "should" question, can be answered *yes* by some people and *no* by other people.
3. Discuss each controversial issue, taking notes of the following:
   a. Where is the controversy taking place?
   b. Who is involved?
   c. What are the differing viewpoints surrounding the issue?
   d. Why are the people involved? In other words, what are the reasons for the differing viewpoints?
4. Select and write a paragraph about one of those issues, using your notes. You need not write about the same issue as your classmates. Follow the conventions of an academic paragraph: include a topic sentence, supporting information, and a concluding sentence. Save your paragraph in your notebook or folder for future reference. Your instructor may also want to collect your writing for review or evaluation.

SPOTLIGHT ON WRITING SKILLS

Newspaper Headlines

Examining headlines for local issues and public reaction is one way to uncover a local controversy to select for your report. Headlines generally:

- Summarize the main ideas of the article
- Use lively language to attract readers
- Are short

One writing convention used to shorten headlines is to eliminate words that are not so important to the meaning of the headline. Words often eliminated include articles (*a, an, the*), the "be" verb (*is, are, was, were*), and some prepositions (e.g., *of, at, on, in*). Omitting these words often makes headlines incomplete sentences, but the main ideas remain clear. In fact, a headline is like a thesis statement or topic sentence: It gives the main idea of the article that follows.

Example Headline

[main idea]   [controlling idea]

Everglades Pollution Plan Draws Criticism

Master Student Tip

Read a few articles in the newspaper every day. Your familiarity with local events, your vocabulary, your reading comprehension, and your overall fluency in English will increase markedly.

EXERCISE 3 Analyzing headlines

With a partner, read these headlines. For each headline, do the following:

- Underline the main idea (the local issue).
- Circle the controlling idea(s) (the controversy).
- Select five headlines, and write a complete sentence to paraphrase each one. (To review paraphrasing, see Chapter 2, page 81.)

Before you begin, study these examples and their paraphrases.

Example Headline 1

main idea: local issue + controlling idea: controversy

Lakeside Sewer Project Riles Neighbors

Paraphrase: Residents near the lake are complaining about the sewerage project there.

Example Headline 2

main idea: local issue + controlling idea: controversy

City Water Proposal Creates Wave of Criticism

Paraphrase: Many people are criticizing the city's plan for water services.

Example Headline 3

controlling idea: controversy + main idea: local issue

Store Owners' Protests Delay Opening of Exotic Exhibit

Paraphrase: The opening of an exotic exhibit is being postponed due to opposition from nearby store owners.

1. Beach Residents Fight Proposed Closing of Library

2. Seniors Mad about Reduced Bus Routes

3. Land Deal Causes Rift across County Lines

4. More Frowns Than Smiles for City Cameras

5. Residents at Odds over Airport Expansion

6. Middle School Moms Bash School Board Ruling

7. Group Slams Conservation Deal

8. Small Beach Hotels Struggle to Hold Ground

9. Battle Continues at Westlake Condos

10. Judge Opposes Request to Expand Phosphate Mining

SPOTLIGHT ON WRITING SKILLS

Learning from Newspapers

To look for a local controversy, review newspapers that you, a neighbor, or your library subscribes to. You can also use a search engine like Google or a database your college library pays for. Ask a librarian which databases might be most helpful. Searching for news online is an efficient way to find and browse articles, but you should know the following:

- You may not have direct (free) access to some articles.
- Some articles that originally appeared in print may not be available online.
- Some newspapers do not have very well organized or advanced search engines.

(For more information about searching online, see Chapter 2, p. 55, and Chapter 3, p. 103.)

EXERCISE 4 Learning about local controversies

Learn more about controversies by completing these steps:

1. Locate a local newspaper by (a) logging on to the Internet, (b) going to the library, or (c) using a newspaper that you or a neighbor subscribes to.
2. Scan the first page of several issues of the newspaper from the last two weeks. Study the headlines, looking for local controversies. Identify two or three possible controversies you might research and write about.
3. To help you learn about those controversies, create a preliminary chart like the following, and locate information to complete it.

Preliminary Chart: Local Controversies

What is the issue?	Where is the issue taking place?	Group 1: Who is involved, and what is the viewpoint of this group?	Group 2: who is involved, and what is the viewpoint of this group?	Source info: author, article title, newspaper, date. If online, also record the website address & date you located the article.

SPOTLIGHT ON WRITING SKILLS

Identifying Effective Topics

When deciding on a topic for a report about a controversial issue, decide if a topic is effective or not. A topic may be effective for one or more of these reasons:

- You were able to find several articles about the controversy.
- You understand the background information surrounding the issue.
- The opposing viewpoints have been clearly explained in the articles.
- The topic interests you.

EXERCISE 5 Discussing local controversies

With a small group of classmates, use the information in your preliminary chart to share the local controversies you have identified, and explain the issues surrounding each controversy. In other words, summarize the information from your chart for your classmates. Take notes about any other issues identified by your classmates that interest you. In particular, identify and discuss topics that you and your classmates believe would be effective for this report, and explain why you believe the topic(s) would be effective.

EXERCISE 6 Reading actively about your controversial issue

Gather information for your report by completing these steps:

1. Select one local controversy to study in depth. Write your chosen controversy here:

   _____

   _____

2. Locate and print or copy three to six articles that present one or both sides of the controversy. If you plan to report on both sides of the controversy, collect articles that will give a balanced representation of both sides. You may want to use the sources about your topic listed on your preliminary chart.

3. Read each article actively. That is, read and "mark up" the articles. Underline, highlight, and write questions and notes in the margins.
   - Focus on the main idea and controlling idea(s) in each article.
   - Identify facts, statistics, explanations, examples, and expert opinions that support the main ideas.
   - Note keywords, topic-specific terminology, and definitions that are provided in the reading.
   - Note names of important people or groups involved in the controversy.
   - Identify interesting or important factual and/or historical information.
   - Look for similarities and differences in various sources on the controversy.

☐ Focusing and Organizing

EXERCISE 7 **Organizing ideas on "information" pages**

Use four sheets of paper to sort and organize information into paragraphs for your report. Follow these steps:

1. At the top of each sheet, write one of the following headings: (a) facts, (b) supporting arguments, (c) opposing arguments, and (d) questions. See the example in the left margin.
   a. On the Facts information page, you will record facts, statistics, subject-related terminology, and other information that may be useful in your introductory and background paragraphs.
   b. On the Supporting Arguments information page, you will record names of groups and important individuals who favor a proposed action. Include claims they make and evidence they provide to support their point of view. Include page and/or paragraph numbers with quotations.
   c. On the Opposing Arguments information page, you will record names of groups and important individuals who oppose a proposed action. Include claims they make and evidence they provide to support their point of view. Include page and/or paragraph numbers with quotations.
   d. On the Questions information page, you will write questions about facts, opinions, terminology, causes, and effects you do not yet understand but need to be familiar with in order to read and write about the issue. Leave space to fill in answers once you have located them.

Master Student Tip

Remember your audience. When you gather and select information about your topic, note what terminology is difficult to understand and what material puzzled or surprised you. Pay attention to examples and explanations that answered questions you had about the topic. Include these definitions, examples, and explanations in your paper to help your readers understand your topic.

Information Page:

```
       facts



```

2. Review the readings you located, including the notes and questions you wrote. Record information onto the appropriate information pages. Include source information (e.g., author's or expert's name and date) so that you can refer to the full source if needed.

3. Share your information pages with one or two classmates who, if possible, are exploring the same issue as you. Discuss useful sources. Take notes about any new information your classmates have located that you might also consider using in your report.

 SPOTLIGHT ON WRITING SKILLS

Interviewing Experts

Finding and interviewing authorities about your topic can be a satisfying and beneficial experience. Your experts may provide information or details about your topic that cannot be gathered from other sources. You can locate authorities on your controversial issue in your campus or city telephone directory, through friends and coworkers, and through the Internet.

In Chapter 3, you conducted an interview to gain information for your essay. For that assignment, you selected questions from a list provided in the text. For this chapter, however, you will identify and write your own set of questions.

Follow these steps when planning and conducting your interview:

1. Consider your topic, your purpose, and your audience.
2. Do initial research to answer basic questions about your topic.
3. Plan your questions according to the expertise of your authority.
4. Plan questions that require no more than twenty minutes of the expert's time.
5. Write questions that are free of your own biases or opinions (but do ask the authority for her or his opinions if they are relevant to your topic).
6. Follow some of your major questions with possible follow-up questions for more specific detail. For example, after asking a question about building permits for a proposed resort area, follow up by asking:
   - "Why do so many people oppose the permit?"
   - "What specific reasons does the opposition give for their disapproval of the building permit?"
   - "In your opinion, what kind of compromise might be reached?"

7. Arrange a face-to-face interview, or interview the authority by telephone or e-mail. If the interview will be face-to-face, consider asking to audiotape the interview and/or bring a friend to help take notes.

8. Arrive a few minutes early for a face-to-face interview, or telephone exactly on time for a telephone interview. Begin the interview with "warm-up" questions to provide background information (e.g., "How did you decide to become a real estate developer?", "When did you become especially interested in the student senate?").

9. Immediately clarify any points you are not certain about:
   - "Did you say that . . .?"
   - "I'm sorry. I didn't quite understand. Could you please repeat your answer."
   - "Am I correct in thinking that you agree with X about . . .?"

10. Arrange and conduct an e-mail interview similarly. Send clear, error-free questions to the expert, and write the expert again for needed clarification.

11. Conclude the interview by asking the expert for additional information or sources that he or she can recommend about your topic.

12. Finally, thank your expert for her or his time.

EXERCISE 8 Writing interview questions

To prepare for your interview, complete the following:

1. Determine (a) what you already know and (b) what you need to know about your topic. Review your information pages, and try to answer basic questions, like these:
   - What is the issue?
   - Where is the issue taking place?
   - Who is involved, and what are the differing viewpoints?
   If the sources you have already gathered do not provide answers to these basic questions, make a note to ask your experts these questions.

2. Plan and write six to ten questions for your experts. Remember, your questions should take no more than twenty minutes to answer. You can begin by asking:
   - What do you know about the controversy?
   - Do you agree/disagree with the issue?
   - Why do you agree/disagree?
   Follow up by asking more specific questions.

3. Share your list of questions with a small group of classmates. Give each other suggestions for improving the questions, and copy ideas from your classmates that may be helpful for your own interview.

4. Save your questions in your writing folder or notebook or as a word-processed document. (After you have finished your report, you will need to attach your questions as an "appendix.") Your instructor may also want to collect your questions for review or evaluation.

EXERCISE 9 Selecting and interviewing an expert

Complete your interview by following these steps:

1. With a small group of classmates, discuss the kinds of people each should interview about your local controversy (e.g., a student government representative, a farmer, a local resident, an instructor, a coworker). Use a campus or city telephone directory or recommendations from others to identify <u>at least two</u> people who might be willing to grant you an interview. If possible, try to choose people whose opinions may differ.

2. Arrange your face-to-face, telephone, or e-mail interviews.

3. Make a copy of your interview questions for each interview. This way, you can take notes during each interview. When possible, record direct quotes (exactly what your expert said) and place quotation marks around the quotes.

Example notes from an interview of a student's neighbor

What is your opinion about the Village Memorial Park?
"In my opinion, too much money has already been spent on the park. That money would be better spent on other things, like our public schools."

4. Complete your interviews.

 EXERCISE 10 Organizing information from interviews

To help you incorporate the information from your interview into your report, review your interview notes. Then, add the information you collected to the appropriate information page from Exercise 7 (facts, supporting arguments, opposing arguments, and questions). Use quotation marks if you use the expert's exact words, and include in-text citations for the expert's words and/or ideas.

SPOTLIGHT ON WRITING SKILLS

Thesis Statements

In Chapter 3, you wrote a thesis statement of opinion to indicate to your readers whether you had a positive or negative opinion about your topic. You then persuaded your readers to form the same opinion by providing details (e.g., facts, examples, research results) that supported your opinion. However, you are not writing a persuasive essay for this chapter writing assignment. Therefore, your thesis statement should be neutral. That is, your thesis statement should not express your personal opinion about the topic.

EXERCISE 11 Evaluating thesis statements

Read these thesis statements from reports about controversial issues. For each thesis statement, underline the topic (the local issue) and circle the controlling ideas (the controversy). Notice that these thesis statements are neutral; they do not indicate a positive or negative opinion about the topic.

Example

Atlanta is divided over whether (club owners) or (the city) (should pay) for increased police coverage in the Buckhead club district.

1. The city of Laramie cannot agree about the proposed plan to spray pesticides.

2. A decision must be made about approving the construction of a $500 million casino and resort area in the Catskill Mountains.

3. There are both positive and negative aspects about the Causeway Clearwater Bridge.

4. Valid points lie on both sides of this controversy, making it likely that the nude beach debate will continue.

EXERCISE 12 Drafting an essay map and thesis statement

Begin to organize your essay by completing these steps:

1. Construct an essay map that includes at least a working thesis statement and topic sentences for each body paragraph. (See Chapter 3, p. 111, for more information.)

2. Underline the topic and circle the controlling idea(s) in your thesis. Review your sentences to make sure the controlling ideas in your topic sentences are connected to the ideas in your thesis statement. Revise your sentence if necessary.

3. Save your essay map in your notebook or folder or as a word-processed document for future use. Your instructor may also want to collect a copy for review or evaluation.

 SPOTLIGHT ON WRITING SKILLS

Background Paragraphs

When covering controversial topics, news reporters try to remain *objective*. That is, they provide background information to help readers understand the issue, but they do not include their personal viewpoints. Instead, journalists conduct research—much as college students do for assignments—in order to report facts and opinions of others.

Similarly, the background paragraph in this report should explain the issues surrounding the controversy you chose. Even though you are reporting on a local problem that has caused disagreement, there are certain facts and statistics underlying the issue that neither side can deny. Provide this background information so that your readers can understand the issue when you explain both sides of the debate in your body paragraphs. However, you must remain objective and not include personal opinions in your report.

One way to begin selecting information for the background paragraph is to consider *Wh-* questions (such as *what, why, who,* and *where*) that require facts in their responses. The answers to these questions can be included in your background paragraph.

EXERCISE 18 Analyzing a background paragraph

Read the following background paragraph for a report on a proposed plan about phosphate mining. Note that in her introductory paragraph, the writer defined the key term phosphate (a mineral with many commercial uses). Study the comments in the margin, and draw lines to connect each comment to the appropriate section in the paragraph. Then, with a partner, answer the questions that follow.

Student Sample: Background Paragraph

The topic sentence stresses the significance of the topic.

Statistics support the topic sentence.

The mining process is briefly explained.

Terminology specific to the topic is defined.

Historical information is provided.

Companies, agencies, and groups that will be mentioned in the body paragraphs are identified.

Acronyms are included in parentheses after the full spelling.

As a plentiful natural resource in Florida, phosphate has had a significant impact on the state for many years. In fact, after tourism and agriculture, phosphate mining is the third largest industry in Florida and employs nearly 7,000 residents (Florida Phosphate, 2002). According to the Florida Phosphate Council (2002), the mining process involves several stages, and workers are trained to perform specialized jobs. First, the phosphate matrix—a mix of rock, sand, and clay about 20 to 30 feet underground—is removed. The matrix is turned into slurry (a watery mixture) and piped to a beneficiation plant to separate out phosphate rock. The phosphate particles are ground into powder and mixed with sulfuric acid to form phosphoric acid, a necessary ingredient in fertilizer and animal seed (Florida Phosphate, 2002). When the land has been stripped of phosphate, the mining company moves to a new area. According to an article on phosphate written by Richardson (2003), in the past, phosphate companies often left open clay pits that filled up with water and useless vegetation. Also, gypsum, a byproduct of chemical fertilizing processes, was piled in tall stacks and contained some radioactive ingredients that could spill or seep into underground water. Richardson also explained that in 1975, a state law was passed that required phosphate companies, such as Cargill and IMC, to design and implement effective systems to restore mined land to useful purposes. Over the past three decades, these companies have worked with government agencies, such as the Florida Department of Environmental Protection (FDEP) and the Florida Southwest Water District Management, to ensure that phosphate mining disturbs the environment as little as possible. According to the Florida Institute of Phosphate Research (FIPR), a mined area must be "restored to a useful condition, and in some cases to the point where the ecological systems function like they did before the land was mined" (2003, para. 3). According to the FDEP (2004), detailed plans for land reclamation must be included in a phosphate company's application for a permit to mine any area in Florida. The permit that IMC has applied for in Horse Creek has not yet been granted by the FDEP. Charlotte and Hardee County residents, who would be the most directly affected by IMC's proposed mining, have filed lawsuits against the company and are educating the public about the harmful effects of phosphate mining. A district judge who reviewed IMC's proposal indicated that the company's plans for reclamation need to be improved and warned that IMC also needs to reassure the state that a problem will not appear in the future (Pittman, 2003). However, the final decision lies in the hands of the FDEP, and the debates will continue from both sides until a decision is announced.

The final statement leads to the claims of each side to be explained in the body paragraphs.

References

Authors were not provided for these online sources, so references are alphabetized by the organization.

Florida Department of Environmental Protection. (2004). *Rules for reclamation and waste treatment.* Retrieved April 11, 2004, from http://www.dep.state.fl.us/legal/rules/

Florida Institute of Phosphate Research. (2003, December 15). *Reclamation.* Retrieved May 21, 2004, from http://www.fipr.state.fl.us/reclam.htm

Florida Phosphate Council. (2002). *Florida Phosphate Facts 2002.* Retrieved April 11, 2004, from http://www.flaphos.org/facts2002.pdf

An online newspaper article is included. Both the date of the article and the retrieval date are included.

Pittman, C. (2003, August 5). Judge opposes request to expand phosphate mining. *St. Petersburg Times.* Retrieved May 21, 2004, from http://www.sptimes.com/2003/08/05/Tampabay/Judge_opposes_request.html

Richardson, S. (2003). *Reclamation.* Florida Institute of Phosphate Research. Retrieved April 11, 2004, from http://www.fipr.state.fl.us/reclam/htm

1. What is the issue?
2. Who opposes the issue?
3. Who supports the issue?

4. What are the reasons for the disagreement?
5. What terms are defined so that readers can better understand the topic?
6. Do you agree with the writer that it is necessary to explain the phosphate mining process? Why or why not?
7. Do you think adequate factual and/or historical information has been provided about the issue? Why or why not?
8. Identify examples of cohesion used by the writer to help ideas flow smoothly from one to the next.

EXERCISE 14 **Preparing to write your background paragraph**

To help you identify important factual information for your background paragraph, review your information pages from Exercise 7. Use these pages to answer at least six of the following Wh-questions. Write your answers on a separate paper titled "Background Paragraph." For each answer, include appropriate in-text citation so that you can refer to the full source later if necessary.

Example

Who opposes the issue?

Charlotte County officials and environmentalists oppose the new plan proposed by the state, arguing that phosphate damages the water supply and the environment in general (Smart, 2003).

1. Who are some prominent individuals and groups directly involved?
2. Who is promoting the issue?
3. Who opposes the issue?
4. What is the issue?
5. What are some reasons for the disagreement?
6. What types of solutions have been suggested so far?
7. What terminology must be defined for readers to understand the topic?
8. When did the problem start?
9. When and how did it come to the attention of the general public?
10. Where do people feel the greatest impact of the issue?
11. Where is the discussion taking place?
12. Why hasn't the conflict been resolved yet?
13. Why is it necessary for readers to be aware of this issue?
14. Why is the issue controversial?

☐ Drafting, Revising, and Editing

EXERCISE `15` **Drafting your background paragraph**

Complete the following steps to draft your background paragraph:

1. Review the *Wh*-questions and answers from Exercise 14 recorded on your Background Paragraph information page. When drafting your paragraph, ask:
   a. What information is essential for my readers to understand the topic?
   b. What information may be interesting but not essential?
   c. Do I need to locate any additional essential information for my paper?

2. After you have drafted your paragraph, consider these questions:
   a. Does my background paragraph begin with a topic sentence that has a topic and controlling ideas?
   b. Have I adequately provided factual and/or historical information?
   c. Should I provide more supporting information to help readers better understand the issue and each point I made?
   d. Have I included a variety of in-text citations whenever I used information from outside sources, including from interviews? (For information on using interview information in your writing, review pp. 154–156.)

3. Revise and make any changes needed to improve the meaning of your writing.

4. Begin a reference page for the sources you referred to when writing your background paragraph.

5. Save your paragraph and reference page in your word-processed document, and print one copy.

EXERCISE `16` **Providing and receiving peer feedback**

To offer feedback to a classmate, complete these steps:

1. Exchange background paragraphs with a partner, preferably someone who is writing on a different issue (if possible). Read your partner's paper. Do not hold a pen or pencil during this first reading.

Save a copy of each draft you write, whether a paragraph or an essay. Copy and paste the text into a new document before you begin making changes. After you complete your final draft, review the progression your writing has taken and apply the processes you learned to future assignments. Also, your instructor may require early drafts to be turned in with your final report.

2. Reread the background paragraph. This time, complete the following:
    a. Place an asterisk (*) next to the parts that are most clearly written. Be ready to explain why they are clear.
    b. Place a question mark (?) next to the parts that are unclear or confusing. Be ready to give suggestions to improve your partner's writing.
    c. At the bottom of your partner's paper, write question(s) you still have about the topic that could (should) be answered in the paragraph.
3. Return your partner's papers, and discuss your ideas and suggestions for her or his writing.

EXERCISE 17 Revising your writing

Reread your background paragraph and consider the comments and suggestions from your partner. Make at least two or three changes to improve your writing. Save your revisions in your word-processed document for future use. Your instructor may also want to collect your writing for review or evaluation.

POWER GRAMMAR

Using Interview Information in Academic Writing

Information obtained directly from an expert can be very persuasive evidence for your readers. Writing conventions for incorporating interview information into your papers are described below.

Interviewee's expertise

1. In a recent interview, Dr. Pat Gondreau, a professor of environmental issues, explained the health risks associated with gypsum (P. Gondreau, personal communication, February 18, 2004).	Clearly identify the expertise of the expert in your essay by using a nonrestrictive relative clause or an appositive. (For a review of these structures, see Chapter 1, p. 35.)

Interviewee and reporting verb (*explain*) Direct quotation	2. Richard Clark, who is a staff member with the College Student Office, explained that "just 2% of the total student population filed a grievance report last semester."	Introduce brief direct quotations from your interview with an attribution signal. (See Appendix 2 for more information.)
An ellipsis mark indicates that unnecessary words were removed from quote. Brackets enclose information added to quote	3. Ed Smith, director of the college's food services, said, "For every dollar you spend on tuition . . ., less than two pennies" are spent on food service improvement on campus (E. Smith, personal communication, May 10, 2004). According to County Commissioner Paul Sent, "emergency room visits could cause an increase [in hospital fees] and this might lead to healthcare premiums rising all over the county" (P. Sent, personal communication, May 21, 2004).	In your direct quotes: ■ Use an ellipsis mark (. . .) to show that you removed some words from a direct quotation that were unnecessary for your paper. ■ Use brackets [ ] to enclose information that is not directly quoting the expert.
	4. <u>In-text citation</u> Paul Luedtke, a representative of the Office of Student Life, stated that involvement in student organizations can often help students "build skills that are useful not only on campus but in the workforce as well" (P. Luedtke, personal communication, August 7, 2004).	Refer to or cite the interview in your paper. However, because readers cannot retrieve the data you gathered from an interview, your interview source information is not included in your end-of-text reference page.
	5. In general, people were in favor of its construction. For example, Mahshid Arasteh, a public works employee, was interviewed about the local controversy (see interview questions in the appendix).	In your paper, tell readers that the interview questions are located in an appendix at the end of your report.

EXERCISE 18 **Analyzing interview information**

Following is a paragraph from a student paper on the controversy over the Memorial Causeway Bridge in Clearwater, Florida. The paragraph includes information from an interview. Read the paragraph and study the comments in the margin. Then, with a classmate, answer the questions that follow.

Student Paragraph: Memorial Causeway Bridge

Interview information is used to support the main idea.

> At the beginning of the construction of the Causeway Clearwater Bridge, most residents and local experts agreed that the bridge and its connected developments would be beneficial to the community. Plans for the bridge and its surrounding area included building a visitor center, a scenic overlook, and a bike and walkover bridge. Plans also included better traffic maintenance, improved parking, and security in fishing areas. In general, people were in favor of its construction. For example, Mahshid Arasteh, a public works employee, was interviewed about the local controversy (see interview questions, Appendix A). She stated that safety improvements like wider lanes, an emergency stopping lane, a bike trail, and better walkways for pedestrians were all expected positive outcomes of the bridge (M. Arasteh, personal communication, December 12, 2003). In addition, according to Arasteh, all of these positive aspects were supposed to attract tourists, leading to "new businesses and consequently increasing the number of jobs available in the community." These positive observations were analyzed by both residents and experts before the building of the bridge even began.

In-text citation is included for the interview.

A brief direct quote (the interviewee's exact words) is included and enclosed by quotation marks.

1. Why is Mahshid Arasteh considered an expert?
2. Where is the direct quote in this paragraph? How is this quote introduced? Discuss capitalization and punctuation used with this quote.
3. Circle in-text citation. Why does this paragraph have no reference page?
4. Underline the language used to indicate where readers can locate the entire list of interview questions.

SPOTLIGHT ON WRITING SKILLS

Body Paragraphs

In your body paragraphs, present both sides of the issue. Develop and explain the opposing viewpoints followed by the supporting viewpoints, or vice versa. When developing each viewpoint, writers often choose to develop their arguments with the strongest reasons and examples of support first, followed by their arguments with weaker support.

Regardless of your organization, the development of each viewpoint should be *balanced*. That is, give equal attention to both sides of the controversy.

In addition, present the controversy in an *objective* manner and do not include personal opinions. Instead, provide facts and opinions of those people or groups involved in the issue, along with reasons that support their opinions.

EXERCISE 19 **Analyzing body paragraphs**

Read these body paragraphs from a report about a controversial issue: Should Treasure Island residents approve proposed plans to redevelop their beach community? As you read, review the conventions of academic writing that are indicated in the margin. Then, with a partner, answer the questions that follow.

Student Essay: Body Paragraphs that Explore Both Sides of a Controversy

The topic sentence indicates that opposing viewpoints will be developed first.

The first reason for the opposition is developed.

Large numbers of citizens in Treasure Island on the Gulf Coast of Florida strongly oppose proposed development in their community. Residents contend that harm from development will hit them in two major ways. The first is loss of quality of life, including the tranquility, safety, and friendship they have treasured for many years (Gallagher, 2003). They fear that existing buildings, parks, and natural lands will be destroyed to make room for this development. Those residents who oppose the plans believe that they have evidence to support their concerns.

A specific example from an interviewee supports the reason. ———▶ In a recent interview with Joan Waddell, a 15-year resident of the island, she explained, "Last month, a beautiful old home in my neighborhood was torn down to make room for a condominium. This is a shame because in many ways, the old buildings are the 'treasure' of Treasure Island" (J. Waddell, personal communication, April 16, 2003). (See interview questions, Appendix A.) Residents have additional illustrations. For instance, developers have discussed demolishing a 50-year-old restaurant, the Pelican Diner, that has been a favorite place for residents and tourists to eat and talk. Daniel Zilka, director of the American Diner Museum, is helping people in Treasure Island to save the diner. He claims that as buildings are destroyed, the island is losing its history (Reinan, 2002). A great number of residents agree with him; they do not want to lose their traditions.

Reference to the interview questions in an appendix is made. ———▶

The topic sentence explains another reason for opposition. Coherence is created by using "the second effect." ↘

     ↗ The second major negative effect residents worry about is that the development of the town will never end if they let it begin. In other words, when new buildings like condominiums are erected, other construction will follow. In a letter to the editor of the *Sun Post*, Robert F. Toth (2002) warns that "the damage of overdevelopment is permanent and leads to . . . congestion, more roads, more taxes, more building and consequential necessities that never end" (para. 4). Consequential necessities include public facilities like restrooms and sewer lines, wider roads, and shopping centers, and they all cost money and add more cement to the area. Treasure Island residents opposed to development cite what has happened in similar places as a direction they definitely do not want to take (Gallagher, 2003). They do not intend to become as crowded as other shore areas in the county like Clearwater Beach, for example, where residents often have to sit in traffic caused by tourists and visitors of the beach. Instead, Treasure Island beach lovers prefer their quiet neighborhoods and local businesses. Some residents admit that neglected parts of their community should be repaired. However, they are absolutely against changing the city's style to attract more visitors and year-round residents.

The reason is developed with an opinion of a resident. ↗

Citation information for direct quotes includes the abbreviation "para." with the paragraph # of this online source. ↗

The topic sentence indicates that the supporting viewpoint will be explored. ———▶ The major supporters of the other side of this controversy are local government officials and real estate developers who claim that every city benefits from redevelopment. After a decision to renovate the 64-year-old bridge to the island, which could cost up to $50 million, City Manager Chuck Coward

The quote is introduced with an attribution signal (reporting verb, *declare*). ⟶ declared that, "it's really been a banner year for Treasure Island with the bridge, new land development, infrastructure improvements and the modernization of downtown" (Saunders, 2000, para. 5). City officials visualize developers' plans for their beach town as ways to generate taxes and provide jobs in the area (Gallagher, 2003). Developers explain that when worn out properties are replaced with modern buildings, these new facilities do not just attract tourists but also improve the quality

Credentials of experts (Coward and Black) are provided. ⟶ of life for local residents. For instance, Harry Black, who is president of the local hotel association, advocates development and sees no alternative to progress (Saunders, 2000). He states that Treasure Island would definitely benefit from high-rise buildings, restaurants, and other businesses. In fact, he warns that beach cities must change in order to survive.

Additional information about the supporting viewpoint is provided. ⟶ Most members of local government agree with Black and are trying to carefully and cautiously change the minds of voters. Treasure Island officials assert that they do not want battles like those in Bay Harbor, Florida, where the vice mayor called the local residents "selfish" for worrying only about their own views about the beach, not the circumstances of the community (Viglucci, 2002). Barbara Blush, a Treasure Island city commissioner, chooses to keep a positive attitude and not insult locals. Still, she is actively promoting a plan that will make Sunset Beach, the most popular spot on Treasure Island, "revitalized, redeveloped, and remade, to keep up with the times" (Gallagher, 2003, para. 34). Proponents of development also emphasize to residents that the city's tax base depends on tourism, and vacationers have many places to enjoy themselves in Florida (Saunders, 2000). If tourists choose not to come to Treasure Island, the residents will not be as happy as they are now, city officials say. The city budget will be much less, and if money is not there, services and facilities will go down. Mayor Leon Atkinson insists that progress cannot and should not be stopped (Gallagher, 2002).

References

Gallagher, P. (2002, October 16). Treasure Island residents are battling city officials to keep their quirky beach community from turning into a canyon of high-rise hotels. *Weekly Planet.* Retrieved October 17, 2003, from http://www.weeklyplanet.com/2022-10-16/cover.html

References are not provided for personal interviews because readers cannot retrieve information gathered from the interview.

Gallagher, P. (2003, April 2). A Florida story: Developers and beach lovers vie for the soul of a small coastal town. *Weekly Planet.* Retrieved October 15, 2003, from http://www.weeklyplanet.com/2003-04-02/cover.html

Reinan, J. (2002, March 20). This time it could be last call for Pelican Diner. *St Petersburg Times Online South Pinellas.* Retrieved October 18, 2003, from http://www.sptimes.com/ 2002/03/20/SouthPinellas/This_time_it_could_b.html

Schneider, M. (2002, December 24). *Cocoa Beach leads state in curtailing growth.* Retrieved October 17, 2003, from http://www.sptimes.com/2002/12/24/State/ Cocoa_Beach_is_vangua.html

Toth, R. (2002, July 22). *High-rises are coming to Bay Harbor Islands!* Retrieved October 18, 2003, from http://town.surfside.fl.us/ policies_sunpost_07-22-02.html

Viglucci, A. (2002, September 3). *Bay Harbor residents rail against high-rise construction.* Retrieved October 17, 2003, from http://town.surfside.fl.us/policies_herald_ 09-03-02.html

1. Why don't Treasure Island residents believe redevelopment is the right choice for their town? Give at least two reasons.
2. Why do developers and city officials believe redevelopment will benefit Treasure Island? Give at least two reasons.
3. Look at the length and content of the body paragraphs. Is the essay balanced? In other words, does the writer give equal attention to both sides? Explain your answer.
4. Circle the attribution signals that indicate the opinions of others. Which reporting verbs show a strong claim (e.g., *confirm* is considered stronger than *think*)?
5. Underline places where the writer explained the credibility of the sources or experts.
6. Place an asterisk (*) next to supporting information that came from an interview. Did the writer paraphrase or quote the information from the interview? How did the writer integrate this information into the essay?

Example A:

Opposing Arg
Major Idea
Sup info
Major Idea
Sup info
Major Idea
Sup info

Example B:

Opposing Arg
Major Idea #2
Sup info
Major Idea #1
Sup info
Major Idea #3
Sup info

EXERCISE 20 **Selecting and organizing material**

You have read and gathered information about your topic from a variety of sources. The next step is to decide which opposing and supporting details to include in your report.

1. Review your Supporting Arguments and Opposing Arguments information pages, and for each viewpoint, identify two to four major ideas to discuss in your body paragraphs. List these ideas in outline form.

2. Identify supporting information (e.g., facts, quotes from experts, examples, experiences) for each major idea and add them to your outline. Include information from various sources when possible. (See the format of Example A.)

3. Number your major ideas, ranking them from strongest to weakest (with #1 being the strongest). (See Example B.) Strongest points have the most convincing supporting information. When you draft your paragraphs, reorganize the ideas so that you present your strongest idea first.

POWER GRAMMAR

Using a Variety of Sentences and Styles in Academic Writing

Most academic writing is made up of complex sentences that can include many words. In addition to the use of complex sentences, academic writers can also use other sentence types for special effects. A paragraph with mostly long, complex sentences can include a shorter sentence to offer dramatic contrast with the longer sentences. Compound sentences can be used to emphasize parallel information and ideas.

Example of a simple sentence	**1.** My major is environmental science.	The basic sentence types are (a) the simple sentence, (b) the compound sentence, and (c) the complex sentence. If you need to review the grammar of these sentence types, go to the website for this book at http://esl.college. hmco.com/students. For a list of logical organizers used to form compound and complex sentences, see Appendix 4.
Example of a compound sentence	My major is environment science, but I also enjoy courses in philosophy.	
Example of a complex sentence	While I enjoy courses in philosophy, my major is environmental science.	
Example of a shorter sentence	**2.** The air we breathe poisons us.	Sentences can be shorter or longer no matter what their grammatical structure.
Example of a longer sentence	Because of industrial pollution, governmental neglect, and the general pattern of destructive behavior by human beings, the natural environment is being poisoned and ripped to pieces.	
Example sentence with parallel structure

The five major ecosystems are parallel in form; they are all short nouns or noun phrases. | **3.** A recent report from the United Nations addressed these trends as it examined the status of the five major ecosystems which deliver the goods and services that support human life and the economy: coastal/marine systems, freshwater systems, agricultural lands, grasslands, and forests.

Source: Wright, R.T., & Nebel, B.J. (2005). *Environmental Science: Toward a Sustainable Future* (9th ed.). Englewood Cliffs, NJ: Prentice Hall. | When presenting more than one idea in your sentences, be sure your ideas are parallel. That is, your ideas should be similar in grammatical form and length. |

Example sentences with parallel structure and parallel development

Parallel adjectives = *hazardous* and *toxic*

Parallel in development: *hazardous* is mentioned first and therefore is developed first. *Toxic* is mentioned second and therefore is developed second.

4. Dangerous chemical agents are divided into two broad categories: hazardous and toxic. Hazardous means dangerous. This category includes flammables, explosives, irritants, sensitizers, acids, and caustics. Many chemicals that are hazardous in high concentrations are relatively harmless when diluted. Toxins are poisonous. This means they react with specific cellular components to kill cells. Because of this specificity, toxins often are harmful even in dilute concentrations.

Source: Cunningham, W.P., & Cunningham, M. (2004). *Principles of Environmental Science* (2nd ed.). New York: McGraw-Hill.

In addition, the development of your ideas should be parallel to the presentation of your ideas. In other words, your ideas should be developed in the order they are initially presented.

EXERCISE 21 **Analyzing sentence length in a paragraph**

Most academic writing is made up of rather long, complex sentences. To investigate the use of sentences in academic writing, number each sentence in the following paragraph by writing the number at the beginning of each sentence. Then, complete the chart to analyze the number and length of the sentences in the paragraph.

Ecosystems and Human Life

Natural and managed ecosystems support human life and economies with a range of goods and services. These vital resources are stressed by the dual demands of increasing population and affluence-driven consumption per person. Around the world we see groundwater supplies depleted, agricultural soils degraded, oceans over-fished, and forests cut faster than they can regrow. A recent report from the United Nations, entitled *Pilot Analysis of Global Ecosystems*, or PAGE, addressed these trends as it examined the status of the five major ecosystems which deliver the goods and services that support human life and the economy: coastal/marine systems, freshwater systems, agricultural lands, grasslands, and forests. PAGE represents an international collaboration of scientists, the first step in an ongoing project designed to measure the long-term impact of human actions on these vital ecosystems. To quote the report's summary, "nearly every measure we use to assess the health of ecosystems tells us we are drawing on them more than ever and degrading them at an accelerating pace."

Source: Wright, R.T., & Nebel, B.J. (2005). *Environmental Science: Toward a Sustainable Future* (9th ed.). Englewood Cliffs, NJ: Prentice Hall.

Numerical Analysis of Sentences Used in a Paragraph	
Number of sentences in the paragraph	
Number of words in each of the sentences	S1 = S2 = S3 =
Total number of words in the paragraph	
Average number of words in each sentence (divide the total number of words by the number of sentences)	
Number of sentences eleven words or longer	
Number of sentences with ten or fewer words	

EXERCISE 22 Analyzing short sentences in academic writing

The following examples are from different textbooks on environmental science. Each paragraph includes short sentences. Analyze the sentences in each paragraph, and then complete the chart. Highlight or circle the sentences that have ten or fewer words. Discuss the short sentences with a classmate to figure out the purpose of the short sentences in each paragraph. The first paragraph has been started for you as an example. You will complete that analysis, along with the analysis of paragraphs 2 and 3.

Numerical Analysis of Sentences Used in a Paragraph			
Example paragraph number	1	2	3
Number of sentences in the paragraph	4		
Number of words in each of the sentences	S1 = 7 S2 = S3 = S4 =		
Total number of words in the paragraph			
Average number of words in each sentence (divide the total number of words by the number of sentences)			
Number of sentences eleven words or longer			
Number of sentences with fewer than ten words			

Paragraph 1: Good News about the Environment

News about the environment is not all bad. Food production has improved the nutrition of millions in the developing world, and the percentage of individuals who are undernourished has declined from 35% to 20% over the past 30 years. Population growth rates continue to decline in many of the developing countries. A rising tide of environmental awareness in the industrialized countries has led to the establishment of policies, laws, and treaties that have improved the protection of natural resources and significantly reduced the pollution load.

Source: Wright, R.T., & Nebel, B.J. (2005). *Environmental Science: Toward a Sustainable Future* (9th ed.). Englewood Cliffs, NJ: Prentice Hall.

Paragraph 2: The Food Web

A caterpillar eats an oak leaf, a warbler eats the caterpillar, and a hawk eats the warbler. This is a food chain. While it is interesting to trace these pathways, it is important to recognize that food chains seldom exist as isolated entities. Caterpillars feed on several kinds of plants, are preyed upon by several kinds of birds, and so on. Consequently, virtually all food chains are interconnected and form a complex *web* of feeding relationships—the food web.

Source: Wright, R.T., & Nebel, B.J. (2005). *Environmental Science: Toward a Sustainable Future* (9th ed.). Englewood Cliffs, NJ: Prentice Hall.

Paragraph 3: Two Kinds of Dangerous Chemical Agents

Dangerous chemical agents are divided into two broad categories: hazardous and toxic. Hazardous means dangerous. This category includes flammables, explosives, irritants, sensitizers, acids, and caustics. Many chemicals that are hazardous in high concentrations are relatively harmless when diluted. Toxins are poisonous. This means they react with specific cellular components to kill cells. Because of this specificity, toxins often are harmful even in dilute concentrations. Toxins can be either general poisons that kill many kinds of cells, or they can be extremely specific in their target and mode of action. Ricin, for instance, is a protein found in castor beans and one of the most toxic organic compounds known. Three hundred picograms (trillionths of a gram) injected intravenously is enough to kill an average mouse. A single molecule can kill a cell. This is about 200 times more lethal than any of the dioxins, which often are claimed to be the most toxic substances known.

Source: Cunningham, W.P., & Cunningham, M. (2004). *Principles of Environmental Science* (2nd ed.). New York: McGraw-Hill.

EXERCISE 23 Analyzing sentences for use of parallelism

Study these paragraphs from environmental science textbooks. For each paragraph's topic sentence, identify and underline the parallel ideas. Then, study the development of each paragraph and, with a classmate, discuss the parallelism used by the writers.

The Case of Saccharin

The case of the sweetener saccharin is a good example of the complexities and uncertainties of risk assessment in public health. Studies in the 1970s at the University of Wisconsin and the Canadian Health Protection Branch suggested a link between saccharin and bladder cancer in male rats. Critics of these studies pointed out that humans would have to drink 800 cans of diet soda per day to get a saccharin dose equivalent to that given to the rats. Furthermore, they argued this response may be unique to male rats. In 2000, the U.S. Department of Health concluded a large study that found no association between saccharin consumption and cancer in humans. The U.S. Congress then passed a health bill removing all warnings from saccharin-containing products. Still some groups, like the Center for Science in the Public Interest, consider this sweetener a potential carcinogen and warn us to avoid it if possible.

Source: Cunningham, W.P., & Cunningham, M. (2004). *Principles of Environmental Science* (2nd ed.). New York: McGraw-Hill.

Types of Energy

Energy can be categorized as either kinetic or potential. Kinetic energy is energy in action or motion. Light, heat energy, physical motion, and electrical current are all forms of kinetic energy. Potential energy is energy in storage. A substance or system with potential energy has the capacity, or potential, to release one or more forms of kinetic energy. A stretched rubber band has potential energy; it can send a paper clip flying. Numerous chemicals, such as gasoline and other fuels, release kinetic energy—heat energy, light, and movement—when ignited. The potential energy contained in such chemicals and fuels is called chemical energy.

Source: Wright, R.T., & Nebel, B.J. (2005). *Environmental Science: Toward a Sustainable Future* (9th ed.). Englewood Cliffs, NJ: Prentice Hall.

WEB POWER

When completing this chapter's writing assignment, you may need to use logical organizers to show cause-and-effect relationships. To review a variety of sentence structures that explain cause-and-effect relationships and to complete exercises, visit the website for this book at http://esl.college.hmco.com/students.

EXERCISE 24 Drafting your body paragraphs

Use your outlines to draft your body paragraphs.

1. Decide if you will develop your *supporting* arguments or your *opposing* arguments first.
2. For the arguments you will develop first, write about your strongest major idea and include supporting information to develop that idea.
3. Write about your next strongest major idea and include supporting information. Repeat this step until you have developed your major ideas.

4. Develop the other arguments, writing about your strongest major idea first. Include supporting information to develop that idea.

5. Write about your next strongest major idea and include supporting information. Repeat this step until you have developed your major ideas.

6. Use a variety of sentence structures in your paper (e.g., short sentences to make a point, compound sentences to emphasize parallel ideas).

7. Use cohesive devices to connect your ideas. (See Chapter 1, p. 22, and Appendix 4, "Logical Organizers," for more information.)

8. Include in-text citation information for all ideas and supporting information taken from outside sources, including interviews. If a point is made in several articles or by more than one expert, include all sources.

Example

The controversy has cost the county over $3 million, and local officials project that an additional $500,000 in legal costs will be incurred by the year's end (Delk, 2005; Yance, 2005).	When citing an idea made in several articles or by more than one expert, include all sources. Authors are listed in the same order that they appear on the reference page. They are separated by a semicolon.

9. Add information from outside sources (except for your "personal communications") to your reference page.

10. Read your paragraphs again, and make revisions to improve your writing.

11. Add and save your body paragraphs to your word-processed document, and print one copy.

EXERCISE 25 Providing and receiving peer feedback

Exchange papers and essay maps with a partner. At this point, you should have a background and body paragraphs.

1. Review your partner's essay map, focusing on the thesis statement.
2. Then, read your partner's paper. Do not hold a pen or pencil when you do this first reading.
3. Reread your partner's paper, and complete the following:
   a. Underline each topic sentence, and circle the controlling idea(s).
   b. Identify the focus of each paragraph: supporting argument or opposing argument. Is the report balanced? That is, has your partner given equal attention to both sides? Write your comments in the margins of the paper.
   c. Place a plus sign (+) next to the supporting detail you found most clearly explained and illustrated. Be ready to explain your opinion.
   d. Place a negative sign (−) next to the supporting detail you believe needs further explanation to be more convincing. Be ready to explain your opinion.
   e. Underline two or three examples where you see good use of cohesion (e.g., logical organizers, pronouns).
   f. Locate information obtained from an interview. Has your partner done the following:
      - Identified the expertise of the authority?
      - Used one or two direct quotations from the expert?
      - Introduced the quotation with an attribution signal?
      - Referred to or cited the interview in the paper?
      - Indicated where the interview questions were located (e.g., an appendix)?

      Write questions or comments about the use of the interview information in the margins of the paper.
   g. Circle any problems with in-text citation.
   h. Give one suggestion to further improve your partner's writing.

4. Return your partner's paper, and discuss your ideas and suggestions for the paper.
5. Revise your own paper, and save your word-processed document. Your instructor may also want to collect your draft for review or evaluation.

EXERCISE 26 Drafting your paragraphs

Look at your essay map and the writing you have drafted for this report. Notice that you do not always need to develop your paragraphs in the order of an essay. So far, you have drafted your background and body paragraphs. Let's now look at your introductory and concluding paragraphs.

1. Carefully consider your "working" thesis statement. Revise it if necessary. Draft an introductory paragraph that will:
   a. Stimulate your readers' interest in the controversial issue you have chosen. Consider how to return to these initial ideas to conclude your report. For example, you might begin with:
      - A quote from an expert or resident. Then, return to that or another relevant quote in the conclusion.
      - Surprising statistics related to your local issue. Then, comment once more on those numbers after your discussion of both sides.
      - A brief historical account of the issue to date. Conclude with predictions for the future.
      - A general introduction to the topic that narrows to the thesis statement. End your report with implications of the local issue in a broad sense.
   b. Provide brief information (one to four sentences) about your topic.
   c. Present a thesis statement that explains the focus of your report (but does not present an opinion of the issue).
2. Draft a concluding paragraph that will:
   a. Remind your readers of the main points developed in your report
   b. Relate the conclusion to remarks in the introduction
   c. Provide the readers with final comments on the topic (e.g., a prediction, recommendation, or solution)
   d. Not introduce new information about your topic
3. Reread your paragraphs, and revise to improve your writing.
4. Add and save your introductory and concluding paragraphs to your word-processed document.

EXERCISE 27 Revising your report

Before you ask others for feedback, review and revise your own writing.

1. Read your entire report carefully, and consider these questions:
   a. Does your introduction stimulate your readers' interest, provide brief information, and include a thesis statement that has a topic and controlling ideas?
   b. Does your background paragraph begin with a topic sentence that has a topic and controlling ideas?
   c. In your background paragraph, do you adequately provide factual and/or historical information about the controversial issue you chose to write about?
   d. Do you provide enough supporting information to help your audience understand the issue?
   e. Do you provide key terms and their definitions?
   f. In your body paragraphs, do you present both sides of the argument in a balanced manner?
   g. Do you include logical organizers and other cohesion devices to guide your readers from one idea to the next?
   h. Do you use a variety of sentence structures?
   i. Do you properly use interview information in your paper?
      - Identify the expertise of your experts.
      - Use one or two direct quotations from your experts.
      - Refer to or cite the interview in the paper.
      - Indicate where the interview questions are located.
   j. Do you include in-text citations when you use outside sources, and are your in-text citations formatted correctly?
      (See Appendixes 1–2 for more information.)
   k. In your concluding paragraph, do you restate the main ideas developed in your essay, relate the conclusion to remarks in your introduction, and provide readers with final comments on the topic?
   l. Does your reference page include all sources referred to when writing your paper?
   m. Is the formatting of your reference page correct?
      (See Appendix 3.)

2. Make any changes needed to improve the meaning of your writing.

3. Save your revisions in your word-processed document, and print one copy of your report.

EXERCISE 28 **Providing and receiving peer feedback**

Work with a partner, and exchange reports. Read your partner's report, without commenting, to become familiar with the topic. To offer feedback, refer to the website for this book at http:/esl.college.hmco.com/students and download a feedback form. Return and discuss your partner's essay.

EXERCISE 29 **Finalizing your report**

Complete these steps:

1. Consider your partner's suggestions and your own insights as you revise your report.

2. Edit for grammar, spelling, and punctuation to reflect your best work.

3. Save the document as your final draft, and print one copy. Attach your draft(s), your list of interview questions as an "appendix," and copies of all outside sources referred to while writing your paper.

4. Submit your report and attachments for your instructor's review and evaluation.

☐ More Practice and Self-Assessment

1. Return to the chapter objectives on the first page of the chapter. Read each objective, and put a check mark in the appropriate box: "I have learned this well" or "I need to work on this." Compare your responses to similar ones in previous chapters. How have your writing skills improved since you began this course?

2. Write a paragraph explaining one or more of the following questions: What is the most interesting thing you learned about your controversial issue? What surprised you? What would you like to know more about?

3. Even though the report for this chapter required you to be objective, you have undoubtedly begun to form an opinion on the topic. Write a letter to the editor of your local or campus newspaper, expressing your opinion on the issue you researched.

4. Read your report once more. Write a one-paragraph summary of the local controversy and the major arguments of the two sides, or read a classmate's report and write a one-paragraph summary of the local controversy and the major arguments of the two sides.

WEB POWER

You can find additional exercises related to the content in this chapter at http://esl.college.hmco.com/students.

Writing an Argumentative Essay

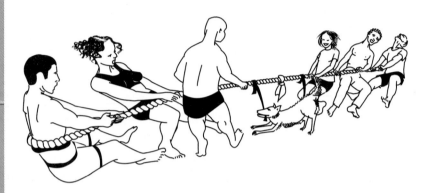

Some academic assignments require you to write an essay that explains a topic and presents your opinion about the topic, along with your arguments for your opinion. The goal of such essays is to persuade, or convince, readers to share your opinion. To persuade effectively, you should:

- **Express your opinion clearly**
- **Acknowledge opposing opinions and show how those opinions are not strong or valid**
- **Provide strong evidence (support) for your own opinion**

Chapter Objectives

Read the following chapter objectives to preview the chapter content. After you complete the chapter, return to this chart and check (✓) the appropriate boxes on the right.	I have learned this well.	I need to work on this.
Follow a three-step writing process to gather, organize, and draft information		
Read about and discuss a controversial issue		
Form research questions		
Complete and refine online advanced searches		
Complete library research		
Practice active reading strategies		
Create and administer surveys to gather information		
Report survey results		
Compose an argumentative thesis		
Create note-taking charts to collect information		
Select support for both sides of the controversy		
Select material to refute opposing viewpoints		
Use language to refute opposing viewpoints		
Learn the organization formats of argumentative essays with refutation		
Design an essay map for your argument		
Cite sources (in-text and end-of-text references)		

Chapter Writing Assignment

Similar to the research you conducted on a local issue in Chapter 4, you will investigate a controversial issue to analyze and evaluate both sides. However, for this assignment, you must argue for one side of the issue. That is, you take a position (a stance) based on what you learn from the information you gather. Your purpose is not only to inform readers of the topic but also to convince them that your stance about the topic—your opinion—is stronger than the stance of the other side. You will present your stance in your thesis statement.

For this assignment, the issue may be a policy, a proposal, or an event. You may do any of the following:

a. Use the essay you wrote for Chapter 4, but revise it to be an argumentative essay.
b. Select a new local issue from your college or campus.
c. Select a new local issue from your city or region.
d. Select a state or national issue.

This assignment requires you to complete Internet and library research. You will also design and administer a survey about the issue and report the results. Your essay must include the following:

- An introductory paragraph
- A background paragraph that includes factual and/or historical information about your issue
- Two to four body paragraphs that explain the issue and its two opposing sides
- A concluding paragraph
- At least two to four in-text citations
- An end-of-text reference page with references for all sources referred to as you wrote your essay

To complete your argumentative essay, you will employ the three-step writing process:

1. Gathering Information
2. Focusing and Organizing
3. Drafting, Revising, and Editing

☐ Gathering Information

EXERCISE 1 Reading various topics

Read the following controversial topics that students have researched and written about for this assignment.

Sample "Should" Questions to Argue *For or Against* a Controversial Issue

College/Campus issues

- Should campus security guards carry loaded guns?
- Should art majors be required to take science and math courses?
- Should the college ban athletic scholarships?
- Should the campus library be open twenty-four hours a day, seven days a week?

Local (city/state) issues

- Should city government raise property taxes to help fund a new recreational facility?
- Should citizens vote for prohibiting smoking in restaurants and bars in the state?
- Should a high-speed train be built to facilitate transportation across the state?
- Should a noncommercial airport be closed and a county park built in its place?
- Should physical education be a required subject in middle and high schools?

National issues

- Should juveniles accused of murder be tried as adults? Be punished as adults if found guilty?
- Should surveillance cameras be installed at random on city streets?
- Should a maximum driving age be imposed across the United States?
- Should legislators ratify a proposed amendment to ban same-sex marriages?
- Should genetically modified foods be labeled "genetically modified"?
- Should international students be allowed to work while they study in the United States?

Beginning Research Questions

To select a current controversial topic for your argumentative essay, listen to the news on the radio and television, read newspapers and magazines, browse sites online, and talk with people you know. The purpose of your initial search for information is to understand the root of the controversy and the conflicting views that people hold, not to find evidence that supports one side over the other.

To begin your research, ask some general journalistic questions—for example, the following:

#1–4 focus on introductory and background paragraph information

1. *What* controversial issue is being argued?

2. *Who* is involved in or affected by the controversy?

3. *Where* is this controversy taking place?

4. *When* and *how* did the controversy begin?

#5–8 identify and focus on issues on both sides of the controversy

5. *What* people are on each side of the issue?

6. *Why* are people divided over the issue?

7. *What* solutions to the controversy have been suggested?

8. *How* will a final decision be made?

In addition to asking questions, take notes about the answers. As you continue to research your controversy, continue to write down main ideas that are repeated, including keywords and synonyms that are used to describe a controversy. Use these keywords to type combinations into a search engine, like Google, to search for relevant material.

Master Student Tip

Withhold forming an opinion about your topic until you have thoroughly examined the arguments on both sides of the issue.

EXERCISE 2 **Discussing possible controversies**

Complete these steps:

1. With a small group of classmates, discuss the controversies listed in Exercise 1. Answer these questions during your discussion, and take notes.
   a. Do any of these issues interest you?
   b. Do any remind you of an issue you find interesting? What is that issue?
   c. What other issues do your classmates mention? Do any of those issues interest you?
2. List two or three possible controversies you are interested in. Write a "should" question for each of your possible controversies.

EXERCISE 3 **Selecting a controversy**

Complete these steps to select a controversy:

1. Review your notes about controversies and your "should" questions.
2. Discuss your selection of possible controversies with your classmates. Answer these questions during your discussion.
   a. Which issue do your classmates think will be best for you? Why?
   b. Which issue do you find most interesting? Why?
3. Select your controversy for your argumentative essay, and get it approved by your instructor.

EXERCISE 4 **Reviewing the Advanced Search option**

Follow these steps:

1. Review the process for using the Advanced Search option (Chapter 3, p. 103).

2. Then, read through the following process conducted by a student. Notice that each time this student refined (modified or slightly changed) her search, the results proved more useful to answering the "should" question about her selected controversy.

"Should" Research Question: *Should gambling casinos be added to Kentucky horse tracks?*

Step 1. Type keywords from the "should" question into search boxes.

Search Box 1. Find results with *all of the words*: Kentucky

Search Box 2. Find results with *the exact phrase:* horse tracks

Search Box 3. Find results with *at least one of the words:*
gambling casinos

Results: Links at the top of the first page seemed to be on topic. Several articles outlined background information and arguments on both sides of the issue. However, many links led to articles not specifically about Kentucky, such as the following:

States Face Big Decisions on Gambling's Big Money
Horse Racing Industry Looks to Expand Gambling
Horse Racing and Breeding Information from the
Blood-Horse

Step 2. Refine your search by changing some keywords and using more search boxes. Notice the changes from Step 1 to Step 2, which are underlined in the following text. Also, notice how these relatively small changes produced a significant improvement in results.

Search Box 1. Find results with *all of the words*: Kentucky <u>racinos</u>
Search Box 2. Find results with *the exact phrase*: <u>racetracks</u>
Search Box 3. Find results with *at least one of the words*:
<u>video slots gambling</u>
Search Box 4. Find results *without the words*: <u>online Maryland
Ontario</u>

Results: Great! Most links on the first page led to articles containing relevant information including material for the background paragraph and major arguments on both sides of the issue. The titles of the first three links were as follows:

Kentucky Ag Connection: Horse Industry in Saddle
over Gambling
Tracks Want Voters to Get Say on Slots
Pick 1: Gamble or Pay More Tax

3. With a partner, discuss these questions.
   a. What are some advantages of using an Advanced Search option in a search engine like Google or Yahoo?
   b. What does it mean to *refine* a search?
   c. Why is refining a search often necessary?
   d. What are some common ways to refine a search?

Master Student Tip

Print selectively. Each time you search for materials, read several articles online before choosing one or two to print.

SPOTLIGHT ON WRITING SKILLS

Gathering Information from the Internet

As you begin to gather information, look for information that is repeated. These ideas are what experts in the field, news reporters, and advocates of both sides of the issue consider important. Following are other reading strategies.

1. Highlight main points and supporting details in several articles. Reading similar material from several different authors allows you to select the best ideas and examples to explain and illustrate the issue for your readers.
2. Search for explanations written in language you understand well.
3. Look for articles on the issue that were published on different dates.

   ■ The most recent articles will help you persuade your readers.
   ■ Older articles may also be useful, especially in your background paragraph.

4. Finally, read extensively to reinforce your vocabulary and understanding so that you can discuss the topic in a clear, authoritative voice. This will help you persuade readers to consider your argument seriously. You might not use all the reading material in your essay, but reading will help you understand the topic better.

EXERCISE 5   **Conducting your Internet Advanced Search**

On the lines below, write your "should" research question for your chosen topic. Remember, this topic must be approved by your instructor.

_____

_____

_____

Now complete the following activities.

1. In your "should" question, highlight or underline nouns and noun phrases that are keywords. For example,

   noun phrase   noun phrase
   Should <u>gambling casinos</u> be allowed at <u>Kentucky horse races</u>?

   noun phrase   noun
   Should <u>genetically modified food</u> be sold without <u>labels</u>?

   noun phrase   noun phrase   noun
   Should <u>security guards</u> carry <u>loaded guns</u> on <u>campus</u>?

2. Open Google and choose the Advanced Search option.
3. Type in your key nouns or noun phrases in the search box "Find results with the exact phrase."
4. Type in the location of the controversy and other keywords in the search box "Find results with all of the words."
5. Scan the results for websites from organizations, educational institutions, and the government (.org, .edu, .gov) in addition to the numerous commercial websites (.com) available.
6. Select five or six articles, and read them quickly.
7. Print two to four articles with information that can help you answer questions about your selected topic.

SPOTLIGHT ON WRITING SKILLS

Library Research

In addition to your Internet research, access the resources in your college or community libraries. Libraries pay for access to databases, which are well-organized lists of articles that are not always available on the World Wide Web. For instance, two well-known databases you can look for when gathering information for any argumentative topic are *Custom Newspapers* and *Opposing Viewpoints*. Another major library resource is librarians, whose job it is to help people with research questions and problems. Ask a reference librarian for help in finding appropriate databases to search, in selecting keywords and phrases for your search, and in determining high-quality resources.

The information you should search for in the library is similar to the information you find on the Internet:

- Major points of each side of the argument and reasons these claims are important
- Facts and statistics that clearly support claims made by both sides (*pro* and *con*)
- Statements made by experts in the field you are investigating
- Results of opinion polls and surveys reporting viewpoints of those involved
- Comparisons to other groups with similar conditions, decisions, and outcomes

EXERCISE 6 Gathering information from the library

Visit your college or community library, perhaps with another student who is also working on this argumentative paper. Consult with a reference librarian about useful databases and keywords, and ask the librarian to help you locate databases and specific materials.

Select five or six articles from the library databases, and read them quickly. Then, print two to four articles with information that can help you answer questions about your selected controversy.

SPOTLIGHT ON WRITING SKILLS

Gather Information with a Survey

You have now gathered information primarily by reading what reporters, experts, and concerned citizens have written. Another way of gathering evidence that supports or opposes a controversial issue is to conduct a survey to discover information, both facts and opinions, from people involved in or affected by the matter you are investigating. Researchers typically write surveys to collect and analyze, or *interpret*, the resulting information that they then use as evidence in their writing.

For example, to collect reactions to proposed changes to the campus cafeteria, you might survey twenty-five to fifty students, faculty, and college personnel as they enter or leave the cafeteria. When you tally the survey results and read the comments of the "respondents" (people who "respond" to your survey), you can predict with confidence the beliefs and opinions of others. You may also find patterns, or trends, among respondents who support or oppose the issue. The information can then become support for the arguments in your essay.

Like an essay, a survey should have an introduction, a body, and a conclusion. The introduction should explain the reason for the survey, how the results will be used, and clear directions for completing the survey. The conclusion should explain the way to return the survey and include heartfelt thanks to respondents for taking the time to complete the survey.

The first part of a survey usually asks respondents for "personal" information (called "demographic data"), such as age, gender, ethnic background, marital status, and/or level of income. For example, in a survey on online learning that was taken on a college campus, the writer thought the occupation, age, and/or gender of respondents could affect their views. To gather this demographic information, the student wrote the following items. Notice the title and the introductory features of the survey.

Survey Questions: Online Learning

Your Opinions about Online Learning

THANK YOU for agreeing to take this survey. We are collecting information for a paper in our writing course that requires students to design a survey and use the results as evidence in their essays.

Directions: Please answer the statements below. Then, return your completed survey to me personally or return it to the E-campus office, Room 426 White Hall by October 17.

Demographic (Personal) Information: Please circle one answer for each statement.

1. Status at the college: student   faculty   staff   visitor   other
2. Age bracket: 16–20   21–30   31–40 40+
3. Gender: female   male

EXERCISE 7 **Beginning to write your survey**

Write the introduction to your survey and the demographic items in a clear format. Arrange three to five demographic items at the top of your survey page. Limit the items to relevant information only. Share your survey with a small group of classmates, and get their advice for improving your survey's items and/or format. Save your survey in your notebook or folder or as a word-processed document for future use. Your instructor may also want a copy for review or evaluation.

> **Master Student Tip**
>
> On your survey, do not ask respondents for their names. That information is too personal and may affect how respondents choose to answer your questions.

SPOTLIGHT ON WRITING SKILLS

Designing a Survey

In some ways, writing a survey is similar to writing an essay. First, you must consider the readers (the respondents): Who are they? What do they know about your controversy? How can you engage their interest so that they will complete the survey? Second, you should consider the purpose of the survey: What information will provide effective evidence for your argumentative paper?

Following are some suggestions for designing a survey that other students have found successful.

1. Keep your questions and statements as short as possible. Usually, a survey should be no more than one page.
2. Make each question or statement as clear as possible.
3. Focus on only one idea in each question or statement.
4. Do not ask respondents to <u>write</u> answers—that is, do not simply give white space beneath each question or statement. Not only will most respondents be unwilling to spend the time writing, but the data collection and especially the interpretation and reporting of results will be nearly impossible. Instead, use the following simple response items:
   - Yes/no questions
   - Multiple-choice questions
   - Information questions
   - Statements that respondents agree (A) or disagree (D) with
   - Statements that respondents rate according to a scale (e.g., 5 = strongly agree, 4 = agree)

5. Arrange the survey on the page so that it is clear, uncrowded, and visually appealing.
6. Give respondents opportunities to comment in their own words at the end of the survey.
7. Plan your survey timeline to give respondents adequate time to complete the survey (but not so much time that they forget about it). Usually a few days is sufficient. You may have to remind respondents to complete the survey—or even seek out respondents and wait for them to complete the surveys.

In the following student survey, notice that the writer followed the suggested guidelines for writing a survey. Various features are explained in the margin.

Research question: "Should the Laramie Department of Transportation plow residential streets after each snow storm?"

The survey title includes the main idea/the topic.

Clear directions are given to encourage people to respond and return the survey on time.

Demographic information is requested from respondents to be used when analyzing data.

Snowy Streets Survey

<u>Directions:</u> Please answer the following questions. Make any additional comments on the back of the page. Then, return your survey to me or slide it under my dormitory door (641 Strutters Hall) by February 4. Data and comments will be compiled and mailed to the city manager before we leave for spring break on February 22. Thank you!

Gender (circle): M   F

Class (circle):   Fresh   Soph   Jr   Sr

Age (circle):   16–20   21–28   29–35   over 35

---

1. How many hours a day do you spend driving on Laramie streets?

____ < 30 minutes   ____ 30 min.–1 hr

____ 1 hr–2 hrs   ____ > 2 hrs

Yes/no questions and multiple-choice items allow respondents to answer quickly and help survey takers compile data efficiently.

2. Where do you live? (Check all that apply.)

___ in a dorm   ___ off-campus

___ on a residential street   ___ on a main street

3. Do you drive to school?   ___ yes   ___ no

4. If you do drive, does your car have 4WD?   ___ yes   ___ no

5. After a snowfall, do you have problems getting to school because of unplowed residential streets in Laramie?   ___ yes   ___ no

If *yes*, why? (Check all that apply.)

___ cannot get car out   ___ streets icy

___ other cars sliding around   ___ streets impassable

___ sidewalks icy   ___ intersections dangerous

___ other (please specify): _____

Most items ask respondents to describe personal circumstances and experiences (facts); the survey gradually leads up to major questions of opinion on the topic (#6, #8).

6. Do you think residential streets should be plowed after every snowfall over 2 inches?   ___ yes   ___ no

If *yes*, which streets? (Check all that apply.)

___ all streets   ___ streets around the college

___ streets near downtown   ___ streets near major roadways

___ streets within a 1-mile area of the college

___ other (please specify): _____

Respondents are given the opportunity to choose "other" and explain their responses when no multiple-choice items match their situations.

Snowy Streets Survey (cont.)

7. Have you or others you know
   personally been affected by
   the unplowed residential streets? _____ yes _____ no

   If *yes*, how? (Check all that apply.)

   _____ could not get to class   _____ had a car accident

   _____ was injured from falling   _____ could not get to the grocery store

   _____ could not get medicine/go to the doctor

   _____ other (please specify): _____

---

8. Would you be willing to pay slightly higher
   sales taxes to have residential streets plowed? _____ yes _____ no

---

EXERCISE 8   **Writing your survey questions and statements**

To write your survey, complete these steps:

1. Reread the chapter writing assignment. Consider your research materials, and decide what information is most useful for a survey.

2. Take out the survey you began in Exercise 7. Following the guidelines for designing survey questions, write five to seven questions and/or statements and add them to your survey. Follow each question or statement with a simple answering scale (as in the previous survey).

3. Somewhere on your survey, thank your respondents and encourage them to return the completed surveys as soon as possible.

EXERCISE 9 **Analyzing and revising surveys**

Exchange surveys with a partner or small group of classmates. Read the other survey(s) carefully, and comment in writing on the following:

  a. Are the title, introduction, and directions clear, and do you think they will engage the respondents? If you have suggestions for improvement, write them in the margins of the survey.
  b. Are the survey statements and/or questions easy to understand and answer? If you find a confusing or difficult statement or question, suggest improvements in the margins or at the end of the survey.
  c. Are the directions for returning the surveys clear, and does the writer make returning the survey easy for respondents? Write your comments in the margins of the survey.
  d. Did the writer keep the survey short enough to fit on the front of a single page? Give respondents an opportunity for "comments"? Thank the respondents?

Return surveys to your classmate(s), and collect your own survey. Reread your survey carefully, and consider the comments of your peer reviewer(s). Make necessary revisions to your survey and save your survey in your notebook or folder or as a word-processed document. Your instructor may also want to collect a copy of your survey for review or evaluation.

EXERCISE 10 **Administering your survey**

Administer your survey, following these steps:

  1. Make fifteen to twenty copies of your survey, and give them to people who agree to respond to them. Remember that not all the surveys will be completed and returned. You will need a minimum of ten completed surveys for this assignment.
  2. Collect completed surveys. You may need to ask respondents more than once for their help in completing the survey. Number each of the surveys as you receive them so that you can refer to them by number.
  3. Tally the survey results. Use a blank survey for tallying your results, like the following example. When you finish tallying the information, you will have a summary of the survey results to use as evidence to support arguments in your essay.

Snowy Streets Survey

Directions: Please answer the following questions. Make any additional comments on the back of the page. Then, return your survey to me or slide it under my dormitory door (641 Strutters Hall) by February 4. Thank you!

Gender (circle): M ⦚⦚⦚ F ⦚⦚

Class (circle):   Fresh ⦚   Soph ⦚| Jr ⦚||| Sr ⦚|

Age (circle):   16–20   21–28   29–35   over 35

---

1. How many hours a day do you spend driving on Laramie streets?

   ⦚___ < 30 minutes   ⦚⦚|||| 30 min.–1 hr

   ⦚___ 1 hr–2 hr   ___|___ > 2 hr

---

2. Where do you live? (Check all that apply.)

   ⦚_____ in a dorm   ⦚⦚⦚⦚ _____ off-campus

   ⦚⦚⦚| _____ on a residential street |||| _____ on a main street

---

4. Copy student comments onto a separate paper. Identify each comment with the appropriate number of the survey (see the following example.) You may use these comments as additional evidence in your essay.

Student Comments

Survey 14: I wish that streets were plowed earlier in the morning. I have a 7:30 a.m. class, and plowing occurs too late for my benefit.

Survey 22: I lived in Denver for 3 years, and I think the plowing here is more efficient! I'm happy!

☐ Focusing and Organizing

SPOTLIGHT ON WRITING SKILLS

Reporting Survey Results

After collecting and analyzing results from your survey, select the information that best supports your arguments. You do not have to report every piece of information you collect. For argumentative essays, the statements and questions for respondents typically result in data that show the following:

- How many respondents are interested in and/or affected by your controversy
- How well-informed—or misinformed—respondents seem to be about the issue
- Whether most people support or oppose the issue
- Why those people support or oppose the issue
- Whether respondents' viewpoints seem to relate to demographic factors such as age, gender, level of education, length of time in the geographic area, occupation, and/or marital status

Here are some ways you can use information from your survey.

- Mention the survey in the middle of your introduction to engage readers.
- Describe the design and/or administration of the survey in your background paragraph.
- Report and interpret the results in the body paragraphs.

When you first mention the survey, indicate that readers can "see the survey in the appendix." Then, attach a copy of the survey to your essay.

Direct quotations from survey respondents can be powerful evidence in an argumentative essay. Although you should not give the name of the respondent whose comment you use, you may use

Master Student Tip

Cite survey results in your essay in the same way you cite interview information. Because your readers cannot retrieve the data you gathered from your survey, do not include this source information in your end-of-text reference page. To review the in-text citation format for "personal communications," see Chapter 4, page 163, or Appendix 1, "In-text Citation: APA Style of Documentation."

demographic data that describes the respondent in general. For example:

- Since more than half of *older respondents* ...
- As *one survey respondent, a twenty-year-old male,* answered, " ..."
- Nearly 90 percent of survey respondents agreed with *the female sophomore* who reported that "..."

EXERCISE 11 Analyzing the written results of a survey

Read the following paragraphs written by a group of students. In these paragraphs, the students reported the results of a survey and interviews that accompanied their research. Study the comments in the margin. Then, with a classmate, complete the activities that follow.

Student Paragraphs: Results of a Survey

The topic sentence introduces the topic.

Readers are referred to the survey in the appendix.

An introduction to the table is provided.

Students calculated the percentages to make their point.

A recent survey conducted for a class project on online learning indicated that the majority of college students and faculty are aware of e-campus courses, but most do not study or teach online. (See the survey in the appendix.) One hundred thirteen college students and twenty-one faculty members were surveyed during the third week of November. Table 1 shows the results of the survey.

Table 1 Results of Survey

	Student Percentages	
Aware of college's online courses	84 of 113	74%
Had taken an online course	21 of 113	19%
	Faculty Percentages	
Had taught an online course(s)	6 of 21	29%

The sentence that follows the table interprets the results for readers.

As shown in Table 1, online courses are not very popular with students and faculty at this campus. A relatively small percentage of students surveyed have had firsthand experience with online courses. In addition, of the twenty-one faculty surveyed, only about one-third reported that they taught at least one online course.

The topic sentence introduces the interviews.

In addition to the survey, students and faculty who reported that they had been or were now involved in online learning were asked their opinions on this type of instruction. The research group designed two sets of interview questions, one specifically for students and the other for online instructors. Each student researcher interviewed one to three online students, either through e-mail or in person. In addition, each

The interview process is described in detail.

researcher contacted at least one online instructor, again via e-mail, and arranged either to meet in person or to send interview questions for the instructor to answer. After completing their work, the class group combined the information gathered in their interviews in order to evaluate the quality of online education at this institution.

The concluding paragraph constitutes a summary of the study.

Results from the survey and interviews showed that although online courses are not as popular as traditional courses, both students and faculty are satisfied with their online learning experiences. However, the research also indicated that a successful college online course requires a great deal of time and effort from both e-campus students and instructors who guide them from a distance.

1. Draw lines to connect the comments to the appropriate sections in the paragraphs.
2. Because the students are reporting the results of their survey, various reporting verbs have been used. Circle the reporting verbs, and discuss the verb tenses that are used. (For a review of reporting verbs, see Appendix 2.)
3. Exact percentages and numbers from the survey results are not simply repeated in the paragraphs. Instead, the results of the survey are interpreted for the readers. In the second paragraph, two interpretations are offered. One has been underlined. Underline the second example, and connect both examples to the appropriate information in the table.

EXERCISE 12 Analyzing your survey results

Analyze the results of your survey by following these steps:

1. Review your survey summary information and student comments compiled in Exercise 10. Identify evidence that can support arguments in your essay. Specifically, consider the following:
    a. Do percentages of some answers support your opinions?
    b. What responses provide details that will help support your argument?
    c. Can interesting direct quotations from the "comments" section of your surveys be incorporated into your essay?
2. Highlight any results you believe will strengthen your side of the controversy.
3. Save this information in your notebook or folder for future reference.

SPOTLIGHT ON WRITING SKILLS

Note-taking Charts

A note-taking chart, like the following model, can help you organize the information you collected about your controversy. Basic questions to ask can be listed in the left-hand column. Relevant information and further questions to research can be listed in the right-hand column. A chart like this model may grow to several pages as you continue to research and take notes on your topic. In fact, you might want to allow an entire page for each question. This way, you will have space to add information as you continue your research.

Note-taking Chart

Basic Questions to Ask	Relevant Information to Note & Further Questions to Research
1. What controversial issue is being argued?	State the controversy and include keywords, phrases, and synonyms that are defined, repeated, and/or used in headlines, titles, and subtitles.

Basic Questions to Ask	Relevant Information to Note & Further Questions to Research
2. Who is directly involved in or affected by the controversy?	Record names of people, organizations, agencies, and special groups classified by age, interests, values, socioeconomic class, ethnic background, political views, and profession.
3. Where is this controversy taking place?	Record names of cities, counties, states, countries, and continents, as well as businesses, universities, and school districts.
4. When and how did the controversy start?	Include facts such as dates and a chronological order of events, explanations of causes and effects, and points of disagreement.
5. What people are on each side of the issue?	List categories (groups) of people on both sides of the argument.
6. Why are people divided over this issue, and how do their viewpoints differ?	State claims made by opposing sides: summaries, paraphrases, and direct quotations that convey conflicting opinions.
7. What specific solutions to the controversy have been suggested?	Include suggestions for action that are offered by both sides of the controversy.
8. How might the controversy be solved?	Include answers from both sides of the controversy and proposed compromises that may eventually be reached.

Study the following note-taking chart with information taken from two newspaper articles. Then, answer the questions that follow.

Note-taking Chart: Gambling Casinos at Kentucky Racetracks?

Basic Questions to Ask	Relevant Information to Note & Further Questions to Research
1. What controversial issue is being argued?	Whether to add casino gambling to horsetracks (Are casinos legal in Ky, but just not at horsetracks?) Need to define: racinos, slots
2. Who is directly involved in or affected by the controversy?	Ky racetrack owners, horse breeders, local & state govt, "Kentucky Horse Racing Authority" (what is this?)
3. Where is this controversy taking place?	Kentucky: Florence, Lexington Turfway Park, Viking Stud, Four Star Sales (what is this?)
4. When and how did the controversy start?	"previous plans that the industry tried to get the legislature to pass . . ." (Kentucky Post, 1/2/04, para. 5) (When? What happened?)
5. What people are on each side of the issue?	Pro: gov/tracks/industry Con: residents
6. Why are people divided over this issue, and how do their viewpoints differ?	Pro: $5 mil/yr in taxes →keep people and money in Kentucky; not go to other states to gamble

Basic Questions to Ask	Relevant Information to Note & Further Questions to Research
	Con: "I'd see no reason for us to take up the issue" of slots, said Don Ball, a Lexington developer and horse breeder who opposes expanding gambling (Patton, 1/13/04, par 2). (Why not? What's the problem w/ it?)
7. What specific solutions to the controversy have been suggested?	Restrict gambling hrs and amts. (Jackson article)
8. How might the controversy be solved?	a constitutional amendment (who votes? just legislators?) ". . . it needs to be put to the voters," said Rick Littrell, president of Viking Stud in Lexington (Patton, para. 5)

1. In your opinion, how will the information written in this chart help the writer draft the essay?
2. Observe the way abbreviations and phrases—not full sentences—are written in the chart.
   a. Do you understand the abbreviations that were used? What abbreviations might you use in your own note-taking chart?
   b. How will this note-taking strategy (using abbreviations and phrases) help the writer?
3. Notice the student's additional questions, in parentheses, which she will research later. What keywords and phrases might she use to find online information that will answer each question?
4. Look at the in-text citations that the writer has used.
   a. Does she have enough information in each citation to use it in her essay? If not, what additional information should she record?
   b. Should she include in-text citations for other information in the chart? Why or why not?

5. In your opinion, which side of the argument seems to be better supported so far, *pro* or *con*, in the note-taking chart? Why do you have that opinion? Why do you think one side is supported more than the other?

6. What suggestions would you give this student to refine her search?

EXERCISE 14 Creating a note-taking chart

You have now gathered information from a variety of sources: classroom discussion, personal brainstorming, research on the Internet and in the library, and your survey. Use the following instructions to construct a note-taking chart that will help you synthesize information from a variety of sources.

Master Student Tip

Take notes in phrases, not complete sentences, for your chart. Constructing your own sentences from these phrases forces you to paraphrase, thus preventing plagiarism. Remember that you need to cite sources even when you paraphrase. To review strategies for paraphrasing, see Chapter 2, pp. 81–86.

1. In the left-hand column, copy the eight questions from the previous chart. Notice that questions 1 through 5 focus on introductory and background information. Questions 6 through 8 help you identify the major arguments on both sides of the controversy. (Remember, you might want to record each question on a separate sheet of paper to allow adequate space for adding ideas as you collect them.)

2. Look for answers to these questions in the articles you have located on the Internet and in the library, from your discussions with other students, from your survey, and from your personal experience. Then, fill in the right-hand column with keywords, names, definitions, explanations, facts, claims, and so on.
   - Include in-text citations for any material you did not know before you began to research your controversy.
   - Use abbreviations and phrases when taking notes.
   - Use quotation marks for every direct quotation (and copy that quotation exactly).

3. In the right-hand column, also write questions about information that seems incomplete or that you do not fully understand.

EXERCISE 15 Constructing a pro/con chart for research

A pro/con chart helps you identify areas of your research that need more information or clarification. Follow these steps to construct your own chart:

1. Begin by reviewing your note-taking chart from Exercise 14.

2. Then, create a pro/con chart like the following:

Pro: "Yes, because . . ."	Con: "No, because . . ."
1.	1.
2.	2.
3.	3.
4.	4.
5.	5.

Master Student Tip

Look for contact information online and in print materials, often listed at the end of articles. If you have questions regarding material you read or would like further information, e-mail or call the author or the representative of the organization. Many people are very willing to discuss issues they have written about. Just ask!

3. In the pro/con chart, include information that answers your "should" research question with "Yes, because . . ." (pro arguments) and "No, because . . ." (con arguments).

4. Analyze your pro/con chart to determine whether you have balanced information for both sides of the argument. To take a stance *for* or *against* your issue, look for support for *both sides* of the argument so that you can make an informed decision.

5. If your arguments are unbalanced (i.e., you have more information for either the pro argument or the con argument), research for claims and supporting evidence for the side you have less information about. Choose two or three questions about the "shorter" side of your pro/con chart to investigate. Look for keywords you did not use in your first search: names of people, places, organizations, synonyms for the topic, terms that are defined in articles, and so on.

EXERCISE 16 **Refining your online search**

Repeat the steps you followed in Exercise 5 to conduct another online search:

1. Try a variety of key words in the Advanced Search option.
2. Look specifically for noncontroversial *background information.*
3. Look for further explanations of the arguments on *both sides.*
4. To look for the *pro* side of the argument, type in the keyword *benefits* or *advantages* along with your topic.
5. To find the opposing view, type in the keyword *drawbacks* or *disadvantages.*
6. Browse sites that may not have appeared in your first search.
7. Print articles that contain relevant, additional information. Make sure to print the complete reference information as well.

EXERCISE 17 **Filling in gaps in your note-taking and charts**

Read the new articles you found, and select material to add to your note-taking chart. As you fill in gaps in your notes, however, do not let your chart become too cluttered and difficult to read. Take a full page or more to list claims made for each side of the argument so that you can clearly see the main points and supporting evidence you collected. Allow room for notes that you will add from further reading and discussions. Do not forget to include reference information. Add any new arguments to your pro/con chart.

SPOTLIGHT ON WRITING SKILLS

Refuting Counterarguments

An important difference between explaining an issue and arguing for one side of an issue is that when "arguing," the writer must identify the major arguments of the opposing side: the counterarguments. That is, in addition to explaining and supporting the claims on one side, the writer must anticipate the responses of the opponent and refute them (demonstrate how those viewpoints are not strong or valid). For your argumentative essay, not only will you identify the counterarguments, you will also refute them.

There are three main ways to refute counterarguments:

1. Show that the facts of the counterargument are not accurate. The argument is *incorrect*.
2. Show that the counterargument is not important or directly related to the issue. The argument is *irrelevant*.
3. Show that although the counterargument is true and relevant, it is not strong enough to overcome your arguments. The argument is *insufficient* or *inadequate*.

The strongest counterarguments are not usually incorrect or irrelevant. Of the three refutation approaches, showing that the argument is insufficient is most widely used. That is, the writer accepts the fact that the counterargument(s) exist. However, the writer states and then proves that the strength of opposing arguments is inadequate and that the arguments on the writer's side of the controversy are stronger, more logical, and more persuasive.

POWER GRAMMAR

Using Language to Refute Counterarguments

Following are guidelines for reporting counterarguments and refuting them.

1. One argument against X is that ...
   Opponents of this stance argue that ...
   According to the opposition, ...
   Critics of this position point out that ...
   It may be objected that ...
   Another argument against X is that ...

   Introduce each counterargument with a phrase that identifies the idea as an opponent's opinion. You do not want to confuse your readers, so be clear about the opposition's major argument(s).

(Continued)

2. Opponents of this position *suggest* that ...
   It *has been argued* that ...
   Critics of this controversy *contend* that ...

   Many of these phrases use reporting verbs (such as *argue*, *state*, *contend*, and *suggest*) to report counterarguments. (To review reporting verbs, return to Appendix 2.)

3. However, *the argument that solar energy is not efficient when compared to fossil fuels is no longer correct.* [incorrect]

   Refute the counterargument. That is, write your strongest argument against the counterargument and indicate why the counterargument is not strong or valid.

   In truth, however, *senior drivers cannot be compared to drunk drivers because being elderly is not against the law like driving under the influence is.* [irrelevant]

   In these examples, the refutation (the argument against the counterargument) is identified with *italicized print*.

   Even though smokers in restaurants may result in slightly bigger tips for wait-persons, *the damage of secondhand smoke far outweighs those few dollars.* [insufficient]

   The refutation sentence functions as the actual topic sentence of the paragraph. That is, the main idea of the paragraph is stated in this sentence.

4. Although <u>opponents of home schooling argue that it has negative consequences for children and society as a whole</u>, *this argument seems inadequate when one considers the increasing violence experienced by students in the public school systems.*

   Indicate your disagreement with the opposition by using a logical organizer of concession, such as *however, although, even though,* or *despite.* Some logical organizers must come immediately before the counterargument is introduced; others must come immediately after. (For a list of logical organizers, see Appendix 4.)

(Continued)

<u>Opponents of home schooling argue that it has negative consequences for children and society as a whole</u>. However, *this argument seems inadequate when one considers the increasing violence experienced by students in the public school systems.*

In these examples, the <u>counterargument</u> is underlined and *the refutation statement* is italicized. Notice the placement of each logical organizer (*although, however*).

EXERCISE 18   Analyzing refutation techniques

With a partner, read these refutation sentences. Each of these sentences can serve as a topic sentence.

1. Supporters of online education state that such instruction tends to be more complete and clearer for students because it is primarily presented in the written form. However, research has demonstrated that course material presented electronically is more complicated and therefore more difficult for students to understand than course material delivered in a "live" lecture.

2. Even though some people resent surveillance cameras, many citizens favor their use because the presence of cameras makes people feel safer.

3. Despite the fact that the U.S. Food and Drug Administration believes that genetically engineered food presents no hazards to humans, many activist groups, including GreenPeace and the Sierra Club, have rightfully stated that the dangers to human health are yet to be seen.

In each of the previous sentences, do the following:

    a. Underline the words that introduce the counterargument.

    b. Circle the reporting verb in the counterargument (not all counterarguments contain a reporting verb).

    c. Place a box around the logical organizer of concession that signals the writer's disagreement with the counterargument.

    d. Place an asterisk (*) next to the words that refute the counterargument.

    e. Identify the kind of evidence given for each refutation (e.g., expert opinion, results of a survey). Write this type of support in the margin.

Example

"paraphrase from expert"   Although a daycare center on campus would help students who have children, *college administrators state that it would present a huge liability to the college.

    f. Which refutation sentence do you think is the strongest? Why? Which might you rewrite to make it stronger? Why?

EXERCISE 19 Analyzing refuting paragraphs

Read the following refutation paragraphs, and study the comments in the margin. Then, with a classmate, answer the questions that follow.

Student Paragraph 1: Should students be encouraged to take online courses because those courses provide equal, if not superior, education in comparison with traditional classrooms?

The counter-argument is provided with explanation and support for the claim.

A logical organizer (*nevertheless*) signals the writer's refutation with support from an expert. [insufficient]

A final statement that supports the writer's argument concludes the paragraph.

Critics of distance education argue that students in online classes are more prone to cheating than those in the traditional classroom. Since there is no one to watch over them during a test, critics state, students can search for answers from previous lectures and notes. In addition, they can even communicate with classmates via e-mail to share answers to test questions. Nevertheless, the possibility of cheating should not deter schools from offering online classes. According to one recent study, the exchange of ideas that occurs when students communicate with each other about possible test answers fosters learning (Jefferson, 2004). The study also indicated that the same is true when students scan notes for answers. In this act of "cheating," students are actually learning something.

Reference

Jefferson, T. (2004). Managing the electronic classroom. *The Educator, 23,* 62–65.

Student Paragraph 2: Should the St. Petersburg-Clearwater International Airport be expanded?

The counterargument (con) is provided.

A logical organizer (*even though*) signals the writer's refutation. [insufficient]

Support for the writer's argument (pro) is given: a quotation and example from an expert.

Additional support for the pro argument is given, introduced with a logical organizer (*in addition*).

The paragraph concludes with a final recommendation in favor of the writer's refutation.

Review how article and newspaper titles are capitalized and italicized.

Even though Pinellas County officials and city planners assert that expanding the airport will improve the overall economic health of the two-city area, a great majority of the population in north Pinellas County state that their lifestyle will be irreparably damaged by a huge airport. Noise pollution is their primary argument against expanding the airport. Mayor Pam Corbino, who lives in Safety Harbor, a suburb in north Pinellas County, is one of the most outspoken critics of the airport expansion. She complains, "Even now the noise of flights between 11 p.m. and 6 a.m. affect the quality of the lives of people" who live in the county (Scott, 2004, para. 5). She also reports on the results of a survey of her constituents who also believe that further airport expansion will hurt the quality of their lives. In addition, homeowners in Feather Sound, another of the communities that lie in the path of the airport expansion, worry not only about the noise but also about the traffic. They refer to research demonstrating that the surrounding trafficways, including I–275, Ulmerton Road, and Roosevelt Boulevard, are already overcrowded. No plans have been made for coping with double or even triple the traffic that an expanded airport would cause (Johnson & Sandler, 2003). Finally, Ava VanNahmen, a Feather Sound resident, speaks for most citizens in north Pinellas County when she claims that the city planners have not explored other options, especially with Tampa International Airport that is just across the bay (Sandler, 2003).

References

Johnson, F., & Sandler, M. (2003, December 15). Community is bone of contention. *The St. Petersburg Times Online.* Retrieved February 2, 2004, from http://pqasb.pqarchiver.com/sptimes/445483481.html

Sandler, M. (2003, November 13). Critic of airport plans ousted. *The St. Petersburg Times Online.* Retrieved February 2, 2004, from http://pqasb/pqarchiver.com/sptimes/445483481.html

Scott, M. (2004, January 22). Town votes to crimp airport's expansion. *The St. Petersburg Times Online.* Retrieved February 4, 2004, from http://pqasb.Pqarchiver.com/sptimes/527711591.html

Complete the following for each paragraph:

1. Underline the sentences that introduce the counterargument(s), and circle the reporting verb(s) if they were used.
2. Place a box around the logical organizer of concession that signals the writer's disagreement with the counterargument.
3. Place an asterisk (*) next to the sentences that refute the counterarguments. Identify the kinds of evidence given for each refutation (e.g., a paraphrase from an expert, results of a survey), and write this in the margin.
4. In your opinion, are the arguments provided by each writer effective? Why or why not? How might they be improved?

Master Student Tip

▼ Your refutation sentence is important because you want to capture your readers' attention and agreement. Therefore, use a credible source from your research or from an interview to support your argument.

SPOTLIGHT ON WRITING SKILLS

Organizing the Argumentative Essay

Organization is essential for successful argumentative essays. In general, the overall organization of argumentative essays is similar to expository (explaining) essays. That is, these essays begin with typical introductions and end with typical conclusions. They also have the option of a background paragraph. However, argumentative essays identify and refute counterarguments. Selecting the most effective way to set up your argument and refute the opposing views depends on the information you collected on both sides of the controversy. Thus, before you select an overall organization for your essay, look carefully at your pro/con chart and the arguments you identified.

Three patterns for academic arguments follow.

Organization A

Develop the pro arguments before you refute the counterarguments (con arguments). This format is suggested if your pro/con chart focuses on different types of arguments or if your arguments are unbalanced (you have more arguments either for or against the issue).

Introductory paragraph	Stimulate your readers' interest, provide brief background information, and include a thesis statement. Your thesis statement should list your pro arguments in the order they appear in your paper. In other words, your thesis statement should be parallel to the development of your ideas.
Background paragraph	If the information is necessary for readers to understand your paper and/or how you collected your data, include a paragraph with more detailed background information about your topic.
Pro argument 1 paragraph	Develop your <u>strongest</u> argument in support of your topic. Include facts, references to experts, survey results, personal experiences, and so forth.
Pro argument 2 paragraph	Develop a second strong argument in support of your topic. Include facts, references to experts, survey results, personal experiences, and so forth.
Pro argument 3 paragraph	If you have one, develop a third strong argument in support of your topic. Include facts, references to experts, survey results, personal experiences, and so forth.

Counterargument(s) + your refutation paragraph	Include the strongest argument(s) <u>against</u> your topic. Instead of fully developing the con argument(s), mention them and explain why they are not strong or not valid.
Concluding paragraph	Restate your main points, relate the conclusion to remarks in the introduction, and provide the readers with final comments on the topic.

Organization B

Mention the counterarguments (con arguments) and refute them. Then, develop your pro arguments. Similar to Organization A, this format is suggested if your pro/con chart focuses on different types of arguments or if your arguments are unbalanced (you have more arguments either for or against the issue).

Introductory paragraph	Stimulate your readers' interest, provide brief background information, and include a thesis statement. Your thesis statement should list your pro arguments in the order they appear in your paper. In other words, your thesis statement should be parallel to the development of your ideas.
Background paragraph	If the information is necessary for readers to understand your paper and/or how you collected your data, include a paragraph with more detailed background information about your topic.

Counterargument(s) + your refutation paragraph	Include the strongest argument(s) <u>against</u> your topic. Instead of fully developing the con argument(s), mention them and explain why they are not strong or not valid.
Pro argument 1 paragraph	Develop your <u>strongest</u> argument in support of your topic. Include facts, references to experts, survey results, personal experiences, and so forth.
Pro argument 2 paragraph	Develop a second strong argument in support of your topic. Include facts, references to experts, survey results, personal experiences, and so forth.
Pro argument 3 paragraph	If you have one, develop a third strong argument in support of your topic. Include facts, references to experts, survey results, personal experiences, and so forth.
Concluding paragraph	Restate your main points, relate the conclusion to remarks in the introduction, and provide the readers with final comments on the topic.

Organization C

State a counterargument (con argument) and then refute it with the appropriate pro argument. Repeat this for each pro/con argument. This format is suggested if most or all of your pro and con arguments are parallel. That is, each pro argument seems to have the same or a similar con argument.

Introductory paragraph	Stimulate your readers' interest, provide brief background information, and include a thesis statement. Your thesis statement should list your pro arguments in the order they appear in your paper. In other words, your thesis statement should be parallel to the development of your ideas.
Background paragraph	If the information is necessary for readers to understand your paper and/or how you collected your data, include a paragraph with more detailed background information about your topic.
Counterargument 1 + pro argument 1 paragraph	Include a counterargument (con argument), and explain why it is not strong or not valid. Use pro argument 1 to refute the con argument, providing facts, references to experts, survey results, personal experiences, and so forth in support.
Counterargument 2 + pro argument 2 paragraph	Include a second counterargument (con), and explain why it is not strong or not valid. Use pro argument 2 to refute the con argument, providing facts, references to experts, survey results, personal experiences, and so forth in support.
Counterargument 3 + pro argument 3 paragraph	Include your final counterargument (con), and explain why it is not strong or not valid. Use pro argument 3 to refute the con argument, providing facts, references to experts, survey results, personal experiences, and so forth in support.
Concluding paragraph	Restate your main points, relate the conclusion to remarks in the introduction, and provide the readers with final comments on the topic.

EXERCISE 20 Identifying an argumentative essay format

With a small group of classmates, study these pro/con charts and notice the main arguments for each side of the issue. Decide which organization format (A, B, or C) would be best for each "should" question, and write it on the line. Discuss your reasons for your decisions.

Pro/Con Chart 1: Should surveillance cameras be installed at random on city streets?

Pro Arguments	Con Arguments
1. Surveillance cameras can reduce the crime rate; criminals know they can be caught on tape.	1. Surveillance cameras are an invasion of privacy; people don't want to be watched.
2. The presence of surveillance cameras in public places makes people feel safe.	2. Surveillance cameras are expensive.
3. Surveillance cameras work twenty-four hours a day.	3. Surveillance cameras are frequently vandalized.
4. Surveillance cameras can keep police officers safe from dangerous situations.	

Suggested Argumentative Organization: _____

Pro/Con Chart 2: Should a maximum age limit be imposed on drivers?

Pro Arguments	Con Arguments
1. Statistics show elderly drivers can be very dangerous to themselves and others.	1. Drivers in their teens and early twenties are the most dangerous on the road.
2. Older people's physical conditions (such as reflexes and eyesight) are often poor.	2. Many seniors today are active and fit; impairments can be corrected or reduced.
3. Special buses and vans are often available for senior citizens. After these people learn the system, they can get around easily.	3. Seniors need mobility, and families are not always available to give them rides. Public transportation is not usually an option.

Suggested Argumentative Organization: _____

EXERCISE 21   **Selecting your argumentative organization format**

Examine your pro/con chart to determine which organization format you will use for your argumentative essay. If you choose, consult a partner or your instructor. Then, make your choice and write it here:

Argumentative Organization _____.

☐ Drafting, Revising, and Editing

SPOTLIGHT ON WRITING SKILLS

Thesis Statements for Argumentative Essays

The thesis statement for an argumentative essay should be the answer to the "should" research question. That is, you state your opinion about the question ("should" or "should not") in your thesis statement. You may also state the controlling ideas you will develop in your essay or simply indicate that controlling ideas will be developed. See the following examples.

"Should" Question 1: Should surveillance cameras be installed at random on city streets?

Thesis 1

Surveillance cameras should be installed on city streets
<u>two controlling ideas: reduce crime & track crime</u>
because they can reduce the crime rate and they allow police to track criminal activity twenty-four hours a day.

"Should" Question 2: Should a maximum age limit be imposed on drivers?

Thesis 2
<u>controlling ideas: several reasons (to be developed in the essay)</u>
A maximum age should not be imposed on drivers for several reasons.

Sometimes, writers include the counterargument(s) with the thesis statement, as in the following example.

Thesis 3
<u>the counterargument is included with a logical organizer of concession</u>
Although there has been public support for restricting the driving abilities of the elderly, a maximum age should not be imposed for several reasons.

EXERCISE 22   Writing a "working" thesis statement

Prepare to write a "working" thesis statement by completing the following steps:

1. Reread the chapter writing assignment.
2. Review your note-taking chart and your pro/con chart.
3. Highlight the major claims on each side of the pro/con chart.
4. Reread your "should" question.
5. Write your working thesis statement on the following lines. (Decide if you want to list the controlling ideas and/or include the counterarguments in your thesis.)

_____

_____

_____

_____

EXERCISE 23 Providing and receiving peer feedback

Provide and receive feedback by completing the following:

1. With a small group of classmates, review each other's thesis
   statements. For each thesis statement, provide suggestions by
   focusing on these questions:
   a. Does the thesis clearly indicate the writer's viewpoint about the
      topic ("should" or "should not")?
   b. Does the thesis include the controlling ideas to be developed in
      the essay? If not, do you think it should? Why or why not?
   c. Does the thesis include the counterargument(s)? If not, do you
      think it should? Why or why not?
   d. Does the thesis contain any grammatical errors that need to be
      fixed? For example, if the controlling ideas are included, are they
      parallel in length and form? (To review parallelism, see Chapter 4,
      pp. 170–172.)
   e. Do any terms in the thesis statement need to be defined in the
      background paragraph?
   f. What organization format do you think the writer should use?
   g. Based on the thesis statement, what questions do you expect will
      be answered in the body paragraphs of the essay?
2. Consider the comments of your classmates, and decide how you
   might improve your thesis statement for your readers. Then, revise
   and save your thesis statement in your notebook or folder or as a
   word-processed document. Your instructor may also want to collect
   your thesis statement for review or evaluation.

SPOTLIGHT ON WRITING SKILLS

The Argumentative Essay Map

The essay map for your argumentative essay differs from an expository
essay map in several ways:

1. The overall organization may change.
2. The organization of the body paragraphs in your
   argumentative essay must include refutation of the
   counterargument(s).
3. The paragraph organization will probably change because the
   topic sentences of the body paragraphs may not be the first
   sentences; instead, they may come immediately after the
   identification of the counterargument(s).

EXERCISE 24   **Analyzing argumentative essay maps**

Review the following student essay maps that include thesis statements and topic sentences. Study the comments in the margin. For each essay map, write on the line the argumentative organization format that was used (A, B, or C).

Argumentative Organization: _____

Essay Map 1: Should the state Fish and Wildlife Commission (FWC) change the rules for boating to protect the manatee?

Indicates the writer's viewpoint and the controlling ideas to be developed.

> **Thesis Statement:** The speed limits for boats on the state's waterways should be lowered because the manatee is near extinction from being injured and killed by speeding boats.

Explains the arguments of each side of the issue.

> **Background Paragraph:** This controversy pits the lifestyles of people who enjoy boating sports against the people who want to protect the manatees (also called "sea cows")—large, porpoise-like mammals that live in the coastal waters of America.

Develops the strongest pro argument (focuses on the history and ease of killing manatees).

> **Pro Argument 1 Paragraph:** The population of manatees has been decimated over the past fifty years, first because they were killed for their meat, but more recently because they move too slowly to get out of the way of fast-moving motorboats.

Develops a second strong pro argument (focuses on the details of the horrible injuries).

> **Pro Argument 2 Paragraph:** The placid manatees do not deserve the suffering that fast-speeding motorboats deliver.

Develops a third strong pro argument (focuses on the value of manatees).

Pro Argument 3 Paragraph: Manatees should also be protected because scientists have demonstrated that they are an important water species.

Includes the strongest counterargument (con argument).

Counterargument Paragraph: Recreational boaters complain that lower speed limits interfere with their freedom and their fun on the waterways. Perhaps that is true. However, lowering the speed for boats will serve such an important purpose: to prevent grisly injury, painful death, and perhaps extinction of a fascinating, peaceful, irreplaceable water species.

A logical organizer *(however)* signals the refutation: indicates the counterargument is insufficient.

Introduces final persuasive sentences.

Concluding Paragraph: For all these reasons, the FWC should change the speed limits on the city's waterways.

References

Kenrick, R. (2002). *Boaters oppose more manatee laws.* Retrieved May 12, 2004, from http.//www.com/news/ 846437/detail.html

Zarrella, J. (2003). *Boaters face new manatee rule.* Retrieved May 12, 2004, from http://www.cnn.com/2000/ NATURE/0605.manatees/

Argumentative Organization: _____

Essay Map 2: Should the courts allow doctors to remove the tubes that keep Terry Schiavo alive?

Provides a strong, simple statement of opinion.

Thesis statement: The State Supreme Court should permit Terry Schiavo's doctors to remove the many tubes that keep her "alive" artificially.

Explains why others must make the decision.

Background Paragraph: Terry Schiavo cannot speak for herself, and she left no legal documents about her preferences for these circumstances. Therefore, she lacks the constitutional right to make the decision about her life (Foster, 2002).

A logical organizer (although) introduces the counterargument and leads to the writer's position (the refutation).

Counterargument 1 + Pro 1: Although Terry's parents want to leave the tubes in place so that she remains alive, Terry has been pronounced "brain dead." Her "life" will consist of lying in a hospital bed without conscious knowledge of the world around her.

Both the counterargument and refutation are based on research. The refutation indicates the opposing research is incorrect.

Counterargument 2 + Pro 2: Some doctors believe that Terry's condition will improve with treatment (Cooper-Dowda, 2002). However, both Terry's doctors and the courts have stated that she will remain in a "persistent vegetative state" for the rest of her life (Foster, 2002).

The counterargument is partially accepted, but the point is refuted as being insufficient.

Counterargument 3 + Pro 3: One neurologist has stated that Terry shows "cognitive function" and can respond to her parents' demands. Nevertheless, even though Terry does sometimes appear to respond, other doctors consider the small movements "primitive stem-cell activity" (Nolan, 2002).

The summary will
lead to a
recommendation.

Concluding Paragraph: Although Terry Schiavo is unable to give her consent to have the tubes removed, her husband insists that he talked with his wife about her wishes and that she made clear her desire not to be "tied to tubes" with no consciousness.

References

Only the first word
(and proper nouns)
are capitalized in
referenced articles.

Cooper-Dowda, R. (2002). The hearing to save Terri Schiavo's life. *Ragged Edge Online.* Retrieved May 23, 2004, from http://www.ragged-edge-mag.com/ 1102/1102ft1.html

Foster, S. (2001). Matters of life and death. *WorldNetDaily.* Retrieved May 22, 2004, from http://www.worldnetdaily.cin/news/article.asp?ARTICLE_ID=34175

Nolan, J. (2002). Judge to rule soon on withdrawal of Terri Schindler-Schiavo's feeding tube. *NRLC Department of Medical Ethics.* Retrieved April 14, 2004, from http://www.nrlc.org/news/2002/NRL11/shiavo.html

EXERCISE 25 Constructing an essay map

Review your pro/con chart and decide what organization format you want to use for your essay. Then, use the working thesis you developed in Exercise 22 and the information you learned about argumentative essay maps to construct an essay map for your paper. Remember to include in-text citations and draft a reference page as in the previous sample essay maps. Save your essay map and reference page in your notebook or folder or as a word-processed document. Your instructor may also want to collect these documents for review or evaluation.

EXERCISE **26** **Analyzing an argumentative essay**

Read the following argumentative essay, and study the comments in the margins. Draw lines to connect comments to the appropriate sections in the essay. Then, with a partner, answer the questions that follow.

Argumentative Essay: Should state or local governments have the power to use surveillance cameras in their communities?

The introduction begins with three short anecdotes (stories) to illustrate the issue and engage readers.

Anecdotes are indented and in italics for emphasis.

A statement of both sides of the controversy is offered.

The thesis statement answers the "should" question and indicates the writer's opinion.

The background paragraph explains the history of the issue [cause-effect].

A direct quotation is introduced with an attribution signal.

In June 2001, a crowd of 100 people paraded with masks on their faces to protest high-tech surveillance cameras in malls and on the streets of Ybor City, Florida.

In October 2002, Pennsylvania State University students rallied against the college's plan to mount surveillance cameras on the campus.

In June 2003, over 300 residents in Shreveport, Louisiana, signed a petition to prevent the installation of a new $25,000 "sky cam" to monitor their neighborhood (Protests, 2004).

For many years, concerned citizens across the United States have demonstrated their opposition to "being watched," but in many cities across the United States, local governments allow police forces to monitor and record the movements of residents every day. To protect citizens' rights to privacy and to prevent the misuse of taxpayers' money, the federal government should regulate the use of surveillance cameras in all states.

Of course, protecting citizens has always been an important duty of the government, and in times of war or terrorism, people often trust the decisions of government officials to keep them safe. After the Oklahoma City bombing (1995) and the September 11th attacks (2001), many citizens were ready to give up some civil liberties to keep their families safe. The U.S. Department of Defense reported that "from the halls of Congress to New York street corners, Americans are calling for more military involvement in homeland defense" (Garamone, 2001, p. 1). Congress responded by passing the "Patriot Act" and establishing an office of Homeland Security. Surveillance cameras started appearing on city streets and in public buildings across the country. Then, citizens spoke out against them, and the controversy grew. In December 2001, the Maryland chapter of the American Civil Liberties Union (ACLU) won a lawsuit for a community group, Viva House. The lawsuit

The paragraph offers a counterargument.

forced the Baltimore Police Department to reveal how it had spent $250,000 in funds for clandestine (secret) surveillance equipment. City officials had to share information with the citizens, and the police force had to discuss its plans for protecting the city, including buying and using expensive surveillance equipment. Satisfied with the ruling, Brendan Walsh of Viva House stated, "Members of the community can now evaluate whether the money is better spent on surveillance equipment or on services such as libraries and schools" (ACLU, 2001, para. 5).

The refutation is signaled with a logical organizer (*however*). The focus shifts to the writer's side of the issue.

A direct quotation (a complete sentence) is used (notice the sentence structure). In-text citation comes <u>after</u> the quotation marks but <u>before</u> the period.

One major argument of those who defend the use of high-tech surveillance systems is that citizens' Fourth Amendment rights to privacy are not violated when cameras are mounted in public areas (e.g., streets, schools, and city buses) because their privacy cannot be invaded in public places. As former mayor of New York City Rudolph Giuliani summarized, "It's all about balancing a sense of security against an invasion of privacy" (Boal, 1998, para. 7). However, when New Yorkers were surveyed on the issue of the growing use of surveillance cameras, 92 percent responded that they were "concerned about threats to privacy" (Boal, 1998, para. 15). So while it may be true that such cameras make some people feel secure, many ordinary people feel like criminals, and most feel uncomfortable, mistrusted, and even vaguely guilty. Why should ordinary citizens have to feel like that every day? Using surveillance might not be breaking the law, but as John Whitehead (2001) wrote in his *WorldNet Daily* online news article, "It's important to realize that the protection of privacy is not simply a legal technicality—it is a basic principle of democracy" (para. 9).

The paragraph offers a second major counterargument.

A logical organizer (*however*) + the refutation is included [incorrect].

A second claim is that the use of surveillance cameras leads to a reduction in crime. Proponents point out that advances in surveillance technology allow police to catch criminals, break up criminal activity, and prevent further crimes from occurring. However, these claims are highly questionable. A California Research Bureau report on the effectiveness of surveillance cameras concludes that "given the important role that crime prevention plays in law enforcement, surprisingly little is known about the effectiveness of new technologies such as

A quote supports the counterargument (notice the sentence structure).

A final counterargument is provided.

The refutation is offered: example, research [incorrect].

Solutions are offered: hire more police, implement neighborhood "watch" programs.

A logical organizer (*in conclusion*) signals the conclusion.

A statement of the problem is offered.

A solution is offered; a quotation supports the solution.

video surveillance to prevent or discourage crime" (Nieto, 1997, para. 2). More recently, the city of Tampa, Florida, mounted thirty-six surveillance cameras with *FaceIt* software designed to recognize faces (i.e., wanted criminals) in a crowd. Expectations were high, but besides a few "false alarms," the software led to zero arrests after a two-year period. In August 2003, the city dropped its use (Dennis, 2003).

One more argument from manufacturers and users of surveillance equipment is that these systems are cost effective, that they are worth the investment because they function like having a larger police force. There is a problem with this claim. The initial investment is followed with nearly constant costly upgrades, repairs, and replacements. In the case of surveillance cameras, an additional problem is the risk of vandalism. In Tacoma, Washington, cameras were damaged so badly by gangs that the police department had to replace them. Then, they had to spend more time and money designing new ways to mount and protect the cameras (Police, 1996). Instead of using expensive surveillance cameras on street corners to keep people safe, more police officers could be hired. Other methods of protecting citizens (such as neighborhood watch groups) encourage people to participate in their own protection without violating their rights to privacy.

In conclusion, if each state passes different laws and each city deals with this issue, too much time, energy, and money will be spent and the controversy will continue. Therefore, the use of surveillance cameras should be regulated by the national government so that citizens' rights will be protected. John Whitehead (2001) makes an important point: "In the end, the real danger of surveillance programs [is that] they leave us thinking about what we shouldn't be doing, rather than free to consider the possibilities of what we can" (para.13).

<table>
<tr><td>

Notice the number
and variety of
references taken
from the Internet:
a national activist
organization (ACLU)

a leftist newspaper

a local newspaper

a federal
government and
military website

a state government
research website

a conservative drug
enforcement
organization website

an online activist
group

a state university
campus newspaper

an online
newspaper
</td><td>

References

ACLU wins release of details of Baltimore Police Department's $250,000 secret fund. (2001). *American Civil Liberties Union Freedom Network.* Retrieved April 4, 2004, from http://archive.Aclu.org/news/2001/n121001c.html

Boal, M. (1998). Spy cam city. *Village Voice.* Retrieved April 14, 2004, from http://www.villagevoice/com/issues/9840/boal.php

Dennis, B. (2003, August 20). Ybor cameras won't seek what they never found. *St. Petersburg Times.* Retrieved April 10, 2004, from http://sptimes.com/2003/08/20/news_pf/Tampabay/Ybor_cameras_won_t_se.shtml

Garamone, J. (2001). *A short history of homeland defense.* Retrieved April 14, 2004, from http://www.defenselink/mil/news/Oct2001/n10252001.html

Nieto, M. (1997). Public video surveillance: Is it an effective crime prevention tool? *Evaluation Studies.* Retrieved April 10, 2004, from http://www.library.ca.gov/CRB/97/05

Police install surveillance cameras in Baltimore. (1996, March). *Law Enforcement.* Retrieved April 12, 2004, from http://www.ndsn.Org/ march96/cameras.html

Protests against surveillance cameras. (2004, February 15). *NY surveillance camera players.* Retrieved April 18, 2004, from http://www.notbored.org/camera-protests.html

Schultz, T. (1996, April 15). Spy cameras questioned. *The Diamondback.* Retrieved April 12, 2004, from http://www.inform.umd/edu/News/Diamondback/1996-Editions/04-April-editions/ 960415-Monday/NEWS

Whitehead, J. (2001). Surveillance cameras signal end of privacy. *WorldNet Daily.* Retrieved April 14, 2004, from http://www.Worldnetdaily.com/news/article.asp? ARTICLE_ID=24250
</td></tr>
</table>

1. Construct an essay map for this essay that includes a thesis statement and topic sentences.
2. What organizational format was used for this essay (A, B, or C)?
3. Does the thesis clearly state what should or should not happen?
4. What questions based on the thesis statement do you expect to be answered in the body paragraphs?
5. In your opinion, what is the most persuasive detail in the essay? Why?
6. Why is the variety of sources important in this essay?

 SPOTLIGHT ON WRITING SKILLS

Background Paragraphs

In your background paragraph, provide readers with basic information about your topic so that they are well prepared to understand—and persuaded to agree with—the argument that follows. Consider answering some of these questions in your background paragraph.

- When and how did the controversy begin?
- What terms related to the controversy need to be defined?
- What are the major causes of the controversy?
- Who is involved in or affected by the controversy?
- What related events have taken place since the controversy began?
- Where is this controversy taking place?

In addition to answering some of these questions, you can describe or summarize the administration of your survey (as in the student sample on pp. 202–203).

Remember, the purpose of your background paragraph is not to argue your viewpoint. It is simply to explain the controversy clearly. Following are sample topic sentences for background paragraphs:

Although two tragic accidents have drawn a great deal of media attention this summer, Americans have faced the dilemma of elderly drivers for many years.

The terrorist attacks on 9/11 led to many new security measures that have divided citizens over how much of their private lives should be exposed.

Floridians approved the construction of a high-speed railroad in November 2000, yet the state has been unable to raise sufficient funds to begin the project.

EXERCISE 27 Drafting your background paragraph

Work on your background paragraph by completing these steps:

1. To begin drafting your paragraph, do the following:
   a. Review the information in your note-taking chart from Exercise 14. (Remember, questions 1 through 5 in your chart focus on introductory and background information.)
   b. Review the topic sentence for your background paragraph in your essay map.
   c. Decide what questions you want to answer in your background paragraph so that your readers understand your topic. (See the previous list of possible questions to answer.)

2. After you have drafted your paragraph, consider these questions:
   a. Does your background paragraph begin with a topic sentence that has a topic and controlling ideas?
   b. Have you described the design and/or administration of your survey in your background paragraph? (See pp. 201–202 to review reporting survey results.)
   c. Have you adequately provided factual and/or historical information?
   d. Should you provide more supporting information to help your readers better understand the issue?
   e. Have you included a variety of in-text citations whenever you used information you did not know when you began researching your controversy?

3. Revise and make any changes needed to improve the meaning of your writing. Add sources you referred to when writing your background paragraph to your reference page. Save your paragraph and reference page as a word-processed document.

EXERCISE 28 Planning and drafting your body paragraphs

Work on your body paragraphs by following these steps:

1. Review your essay map, and answer the following questions:
   a. Are the topic sentences directly related to the thesis statement?
   b. Are the topic sentences organized in a logical manner (e.g., from strongest to weakest argument)?
   c. Is your chosen organization format still the best format for your essay?

2. Make revisions to your essay map where appropriate.

3. Review your note-taking and pro/con charts to help you identify major arguments on both sides of the controversy.

4. Report the results of your survey in the body paragraphs. Direct quotations from survey respondents can be powerful evidence in your arguments.

5. Draft your body paragraphs, following the conventions of academic writing you have practiced so far in this course:

   a. Write topic sentences with clear main ideas and controlling idea(s).

   b. Provide clear, convincing explanations and examples to persuade your readers.

   c. Summarize and paraphrase ideas as supporting points in your paper.

   d. Use logical organizers to improve the coherence within and between your paragraphs.

   e. In addition to logical organizers, include other cohesion devices (like repetition of key words and phrases, different forms of a word, and pronouns) to help your readers understand the connection of ideas.

   f. Use appropriate structures that control the strength of opinions. (To review these structures, see Chapter 3, pp. 134–136.)

   g. Use refutation language when refuting counterarguments.

   h. Include in-text citation with any information you did not know when you began researching your controversy, and use a variety of attribution signals.

   j. Provide information to explain the credibility of your outside sources.

   k. Conclude with a statement that highlights your point of view.

6. Add and save all outside source information to your reference page.

7. Add and save your body paragraphs to your word-processed document. Your instructor may also want to collect a copy of your writing for review or evaluation.

 EXERCISE 29 **Providing and receiving peer feedback**

Complete the following steps:

1. Exchange papers and essay maps with a partner. At this point, you should have a background and body paragraphs. Review your

partner's essay map, focusing on the thesis statement. Then, read your partner's paper. Do not hold a pen or pencil when you do this first reading.

2. Reread the paper. This time, on your partner's paper, do the following:
   a. Underline each topic sentence and circle the controlling idea(s).
   b. Identify the organization format used (A, B, or C), and write that at the top of the paper.
   c. Place a plus sign (+) next to the pro argument you found most convincing (most clearly explained and illustrated). Be ready to explain your opinion.
   d. Place a negative sign (−) next to any pro argument you believe needs further explanation to be more convincing. Be ready to explain your opinion.
   e. Place an asterisk (*) next to examples of refutation language. If you have questions about the use of this language, write them in the margin.
   f. Underline two or three examples of good use of cohesion (e.g., logical organizers, pronouns).
   g. Locate information obtained from a survey. Has your partner done all the following?
      - *Described the design and/or administration of the survey in the background paragraph*
      - *Reported and interpreted the results of the survey in the body paragraphs*
      - *Used one or two direct quotations from a respondent to support a viewpoint and introduced each with an attribution signal*
      - *Referred to or cited the survey in the paper*
      - *Indicated where the survey is located (e.g., an appendix)*

   Write questions or comments about the use of the survey information in the margins of the paper.
   h. Circle any problems with in-text citation.
   i. Give one suggestion to further improve your partner's writing.
3. Return your partner's paper, and discuss your ideas and suggestions. Revise your own paper, and save your word-processed document. Your instructor may also want to collect your draft for review or evaluation.

SPOTLIGHT ON WRITING SKILLS

Introductory and Concluding Paragraphs

The introductory and concluding paragraphs of an argumentative essay can differ slightly from the other introductions and conclusions you have written during this course. For example, in addition to the other introductory techniques you have learned and practiced, you may choose to use one of the following techniques:

1. If the controversy you selected is local, you might choose to begin your essay with an anecdote (a brief story) directly related to the issue.
2. For regional or national issues, you might begin with a question that encourages readers to look more closely at the controversy. Then, you might briefly answer that question with information about the issue.
3. You might begin with a statement about a larger issue that directly relates to your issue.
4. You can mention your survey.

The introductory paragraph should do the following:

a. Engage your readers
b. Provide brief background information about your topic
c. Suggest your stance on the controversy in your thesis statement. Your thesis may also mention the strongest counterargument of the opposition (See pp. 223–224 about thesis statements.)

The concluding paragraph of an argumentative essay is the writer's last opportunity to persuade readers. Therefore, the conclusion must be strong. In addition to briefly summarizing your side of the argument, you should do one or more of the following:

a. Make a recommendation
b. Suggest a compromise between your stance and the opposition's stance
c. Offer a solution to the issue
d. Predict the effects of the implementation of one or both sides of the argument

EXERCISE 30 Analyzing paragraphs

*Read the sample introductory and concluding paragraphs for this "should"
research question:* Should Florida citizens vote for the "bullet train"?
*Study the comments in the margin. Then, with a classmate, answer the
questions that follow.*

Introductory Paragraph 1: Pro Argument (Yes, because . . .)

The essay begins
with an anecdote.

The story moves
from past to present
(twenty years later).

An earlier solution is
identified: "a bullet
train."

A contrast is
presented—lack of
money causes
reconsideration.

The thesis states the
writer's opinion.

The conclusion is
introduced with a
logical organizer.

A summary of the
reasons is included:
comfort,
convenience, boost
to economy.

The conclusion ends
with a prediction.

The first time I visited Florida in the summer of 1983,
I remember an incredible day when my boyfriend and I watched
the sun rise on the east coast and the sun set on the west coast.
After a morning walk on Daytona Beach, we drove approximately
100 miles west to St. Petersburg. Cruising with the top down in
our rented Thunderbird, we encountered very little traffic on the
interstate and were swimming in the Gulf of Mexico by early
afternoon. Over twenty years later, that scenario is a distant
dream. I-4, the infamous east-west route across Central Florida, is
now constantly congested and undergoing construction. After
years of studying this problem, the 2002 Florida legislature asked
citizens to voice their opinions on building a high-speed railroad,
and voters passed the "bullet train" initiative. However, due to
funding problems, the governor has recently asked Floridians to
reconsider this vital project even though it was clear from the
start that construction would be expensive. Florida voters should
maintain their decision to add a high-speed railroad as a sound
investment for the future of their state.

Concluding Paragraph 1: Pro Argument (Yes, because . . .)

In short, the voters have spoken, and elected officials need
to listen. A high-speed railroad across the state will provide
Florida residents and visitors a comfortable, safe ride to popular
destinations including theme parks, nature trails, and coastal
areas. Convenient travel across the state will attract vacationers
and boost Florida's economy. The environment will also benefit
as energy-efficient technology replaces the exhaust of backed-up
traffic on I-4. And who knows? The fantasy of breakfast
overlooking the Atlantic and dinner on the Gulf of Mexico may
become a reality once more.

Statements of a
larger problem
begin the essay.

The problem is
narrowed to Florida
(engages readers).

An earlier solution
is indicated and a
contrast is
presented—lack of
money.

The thesis states
the writer's opinion.

Introductory Paragraph 2: Con Argument (No, because . . .)

America is one of the most advanced countries in the world; however, a great surprise to immigrants and visitors is its poor public transportation system. Buses and subways are used in populated urban areas, but in most states where cities are spread apart, Americans crowd the roads in their cars, trucks, and SUVs. In Florida, tourists and winter residents add to the local traffic, and congestion is the predictable result. A recent initiative to construct a high-speed "bullet train" across the state seemed to be the perfect solution to annoying traffic jams, and excited voters passed this proposal in 2002. However, since then, the state government studied the reality of funding this project and concluded that the high costs of constructing and maintaining a high-speed train outweigh the complaints of impatient drivers. At a time when the state is struggling with a limited budget, citizens should listen to the advice of authorities and reject the idea of the proposed railroad.

A logical organizer
(*to conclude*) signals
the conclusion.

A summary is
included.

The conclusion ends
with a
recommendation.

Concluding Paragraph 2: Con Argument (No, because . . .)

To conclude, there are times when the state government needs to exercise its power to make decisions with the good of all its citizens. The option of a high-speed railroad is a perfect example of a choice made by voters who are looking ahead to enjoying the finished product without thinking through the complex process. The government is right to question the need for a bullet train when funding is desperately needed for education at all levels and health care for all ages. The citizens of Florida should support their elected officials in this matter.

1. Draw lines to connect the comments to the appropriate sentence(s) in the paragraphs.

2. What introductory technique was used for each introduction? Which do you prefer? Why?

_____

_____

3. Underline each thesis statement. What arguments and supporting information do you expect to be developed in the body of these essays?

_____

_____

4. What strategy was used to end each conclusion (e.g., make a recommendation, suggest a compromise, offer a solution, or predict the effects)? Which do you believe is most effective? Why?

_____

_____

_____

EXERCISE 3i Drafting your paragraphs

Complete the following to draft your paragraphs:

1. Look at your essay map and the writing you have already drafted for this essay. Consider your "working" thesis statement. Revise it if necessary. Then, draft an introductory paragraph that does the following:

   a. Stimulates your readers' interest in the controversial issue you have chosen. Consider how to return to these initial ideas to conclude your report. For example, you might begin with one of these:

- A quote from an expert or resident and return to that or another relevant quote in the conclusion
- Surprising statistics related to your issue and comment once more on those numbers after your discussion of both sides
- An anecdote (a brief story) directly related to the issue
- A question that encourages your readers to look more closely at the controversy
- A statement about a larger issue that relates directly to your issue
- Brief information about your survey

    b. Provides brief information (one to four sentences) about your topic

    c. Presents a thesis statement that answers your "should" research question

2. Draft a concluding paragraph that does the following:
       a. Reminds readers of the main points developed in your essay
       b. Relates the conclusion to remarks in the introduction
       c. Provides readers with final comments on the topic (e.g., makes a recommendation, suggests a compromise, offers a solution, or predicts the effects)
       d. Does not introduce new information about your topic

3. Reread your paragraphs, and revise if needed to improve your writing. Then, add and save your introductory and concluding paragraphs to your word-processed document, and print three copies.

EXERCISE 32 **Providing and receiving peer feedback**

Work in a group of two to four students. Give each person in the group a copy of your essay. Each group member will serve as an expert reviewer and focus on the same (one) aspect of writing for each essay. (In smaller groups, some students may focus on two aspects. In larger groups, students can collaborate on the same aspect.)

Read your classmates' papers, without commenting, to become familiar with each topic. To offer feedback, refer to the website for this book at http://esl.college.hmco.com/students and download a feedback form. When you have offered written feedback, return and discuss your classmates' papers.

EXERCISE 33 Finalizing your essay

Consider your classmates' suggestions and your own insights as you revise your essay. Edit for grammar, spelling, and punctuation to reflect your best work. Save the document as your final draft, and print one copy. Attach your draft(s), one copy of your survey as an appendix, and copies of all outside sources referred to as you wrote your paper. Submit your paper and attachments for your instructor's review and evaluation.

☐ More Practice and Self-Assessment

1. Write a refutation paragraph arguing *against* the position you took in your argumentative essay. In other words, respond to one of your main arguments as if you were the opposition.
2. Write one paragraph of advice to other students who will complete this argumentative writing assignment. Write clear suggestions for researching a controversial topic, analyzing pros and cons, taking and supporting a position, and refuting opposing viewpoints.

WEB POWER

You can find additional exercises related to the content in this chapter at **http://esl.college.hmco.com/students**.

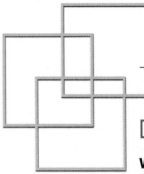

Appendix 1

☐ In-text Citation: APA Style of Documentation

When you include information from outside sources in your paper, you must let your readers know where this information came from. In other words, you must cite outside sources. Different academic disciplines use different systems to cite sources. This textbook focuses on the APA (American Psychological Association) style. The following information will guide you when incorporating citations within your paper (using in-text citations). You may also refer to the website for this book at http://esl.college.hmco.com/students.

For each in-text citation, you must include (a) the name of the author whose work you referred to and (b) the year of publication. This information is needed for both paraphrasing and quoting. Following are two basic ways to use APA style in-text citation for paraphrasing and quoting:

In-text Citation with Paraphrases: Using Ideas (But Not the Words) of the Author	
According to Hudson (2004), a research attorney for the First Amendment Center, schools are increasingly regulating what students may wear through dress-code and uniform policies, some of which may be unconstitutional.	▪ Introduce a paraphrase with the author's last name and an attribution signal. Place the year of publication in parentheses immediately after the name. ▪ If the attribution phrase uses a comma, the punctuation goes after the citation in parentheses. (See Appendix 2 for more information about attribution signals.)
The Fourth Amendment is not clear when a foreign government searches an American citizen with the assistance of the U.S. (Jones, 2005).	▪ If the paraphrase does not include the author's name, the last name and year of publication are placed in parentheses at the end of the sentence. ▪ A comma comes between the name and the year. ▪ The punctuation at the end of the sentence comes after the citation in parentheses.

In-text Citation with Quotations: Using Ideas and Words of the Author

In his article, Sinnott (2004) declared, "There are diseases we cannot know are incubating, ready to break out. I worry not just that we will see more, but that their severity will increase" (p. 15). The National Institute of Allergy and Infectious Diseases (2002) defines anthrax as "an acute infectious disease caused by the spore-forming, rod-shaped bacterium *Bacillus anthracis*" (para. 1).	▪ Introduce the quote with an attribution signal and the author's last name. Also, place the year in parentheses after the name, put quotation marks around the quote, and place the page number of the original quote in parentheses at the end of the sentence. ▪ When a document does not contain page numbers, use the paragraph number in which the quotation occurs. ▪ Abbreviations are used for page and paragraph numbers: p. = 1 page, pp. = more than 1 page, para. = 1 or more paragraphs. ▪ Punctuation at the end of the sentence comes after the citation in parentheses.
According to a *New York Times* article, "249 individual cases of SARS could all be traced to one man. . . . Of those infected, 214 were medical personnel or health-care workers" (Gondreau, 2003, p. 6).	▪ If the sentence does not include the author's name, then after the quotation, in parentheses, include the author's last name, year of publication, and page/paragraph number on which the quotation occurs. However, if possible, include the name of the author in the sentence. ▪ A comma comes between the author's last name, the year, and the page/paragraph number. ▪ Punctuation at the end of the sentence comes after the citation in parentheses.

Following are examples of in-text citation (both paraphrasing and quoting) for various sources:

Documented cases of AIDS occurred in the early 1980s (Pearson, 2003).	**1.** One author
At the Constitutional Convention in Philadelphia, George Washington suggested adding a list of civil liberties, called the Bill of Rights (Janda, Berry, & Goldman, 2003).	**2.** Two or more authors List all authors in your citation. A comma and an ampersand (&) separate the last two names.
"Aerosolized droplets that are exhaled when a patient breathes and bodily secretions from an infected person both spread the disease" (CDC, 2004, para. 4). The phosphate particles are ground into powder and mixed with sulfuric acid to form phosphoric acid, a necessary ingredient in fertilizer and animal seed (Florida Phosphate Facts, 2002).	**3.** No author identified Give the organization name or the first few words of the title in your citation.
In his experience, Dr. Morgan has seen that students "form collaborative bonds witnessed in their heartfelt goodbyes at the close of each semester" (K. Morgan, personal communication, October 26, 2004).	**4.** Personal communication (e.g., interview, survey)
Some precautionary measures for medical personnel include washing hands regularly, wearing and frequently discarding disposable gowns and gloves, and wearing eye protection (Nguyen, n.d.).	**5.** Source with no date Electronic sources often lack author names and/or dates. If the electronic source does not include an author, use the format for "no author identified" illustrated above. If the electronic source does not include a publication date, see the example. *Note:* "n.d." indicates "no date."

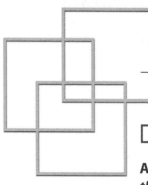

Appendix 2

Attribution Signals to Cite Sources

Attribution signals (like *According to Smith* and *Jones explained that*) help you integrate outside sources into your paper. These words and phrases are called attribution signals because they signal the reader that the ideas and information presented are attributed—or belong—to someone else (not the writer). Following are two types of attribution signals that can be used to introduce both quoting and paraphrasing in your essays.

A. Reporting Verbs as Attribution Signals

A "quotation" with a reporting verb (*reported*) and the expert's last name The expert's last name and a reporting verb (*pointed out*) with a paraphrase	**1.** "The Vermont law violates the federal Commerce Clause, which states that only Congress can regulate interstate commerce," reported Waddell (2005). Waddell (2005) pointed out that communication on the Internet is considered interstate commerce, and therefore, the Vermont law violates the Commerce Clause.	Reporting verbs can be used to introduce a quote or a paraphrase.
	2. note assert think declare suggest report feel explain mention illustrate point out discover express argue state show imply confirm infer demonstrate propose prove report conclude present emphasize allege attest claim find	You can choose from a variety of reporting verbs to introduce your quote or paraphrase.

3. Your expert might be *proving* a point, *reporting* a fact, or *expressing* an opinion. If you have clear details (e.g., facts, explanations) to support the claim, you might use the verb *confirm* or *prove*. If the supporting information is not very strong, you might use *indicate* or *suggest*.	You select a reporting verb based on: (a) The context (b) The strength of the claim
4. Burman (2005) <u>reported</u> that the Vermont law burdened the First Amendment and was not narrowly tailored.	The past tense is usually used in the reporting verb.
5. Survey results <u>demonstrate</u> that the majority of citizens cannot identify the first ten amendments of the U.S. Constitution (Smith, 2004).	Present tense is used when presenting research results or when reporting "general truth."
6. Drew Wade (2004), a spokesman for the U.S. Department of Justice, <u>said</u>, "The important thing to realize is that the United States can't be a party to any convention that abridges a constitutional protection."	When reporting verbs are used with *quotes*, (a) a comma separates the reporting verb and the quote and (b) quotation marks are placed around the quote.
7. Monk (2004) <u>explained</u> that the First Amendment reveals a complex set of laws written to protect the rights of citizens.	When reporting verbs are used with *paraphrases*, a noun clause is usually included as the direct object. Notice that (a) a comma does not separate the reporting verb and the noun clause and (b) quotation marks are not used.

8. Three Cedarville school board members who proposed restrictions on the Harry Potter series <u>said</u> that they <u>felt</u> the books <u>prompted</u> children to disobey authority. (The original quote was, "We <u>feel</u> the Harry Potter books <u>prompt</u> children to disobey authority.")	Within the noun clause, the verb changes to match the verb tense of the reporting verb. <u>original tense</u> <u>revised tense in noun clause</u> simple present → simple past *(report)* *(reported)* simple past → past perfect *(reported)* *(had reported)* the modal → the modal *will* *would* *(will report)* *(would report)* the modal → the modal *can* *could* *(can report)* *(could report)*
9. The school board <u>announced</u> that students <u>need</u> parental permission to check out a Harry Potter book from the school library.	A verb tense change in the clause does not occur if the writer thinks the change will affect the meaning of the sentence. In this example, the present tense verb indicates that students still need permission.

B. Phrases as Attribution Signals

1. According to Stevenson (2005), . . . As Klingaman (2004) emphasized in her book, ". . ." Based on Wald's (2004) research presented in *Shortcomings of the Constitution*, . . . In the words of Snell (2005), ". . ."	Certain phrases can be used to introduce a quote or a paraphrase.

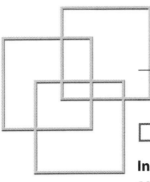

Appendix 3

☐ End-of-Text References: APA Style of Documentation

In addition to providing in-text citations, provide a list of all the sources you used when writing your paper. This reference list, which occurs on a separate page at the end of your paper, provides readers with information to retrieve original sources, if desired. There are strict rules to follow about capitalization, punctuation, and formatting. The following list will guide you when creating your reference list, using the APA style of documentation. You might also want to refer to the website for this book at http://esl.college.hmco.com/students.

1. Put your reference list on a separate page at the end of your paper.
2. Center a heading (*References*) at the top of the page.
3. Type the first line of each reference at the left-hand margin, but indent all other lines (about 1/2 inch, five spaces, or one tab).
4. Use each author's last name and the initial of her or his first name (Last, F.).
5. Alphabetize your list (e.g., by the authors' last names) (Adams, S.; Zoon, P.).
6. List the names of more than one author in the order they appear on the original source, and place an ampersand (&) between the last two names (Duncan, L., & Atkins, G.).
7. If the author is not identified, begin the reference with the title of the document.
8. When no publication date is identified, use n.d., the abbreviation for "no date."
9. Use double spacing throughout your list.
10. Pay careful attention to capitalization in the titles (see the examples that follow).
11. Pay particular attention to punctuation (see the examples).

The following sample reference list uses APA documentation style (except for double-spacing in order to conserve space). Study the entries carefully for capitalization and punctuation. For your own reference page, copy the formatting of these entries exactly.

Format	Source
References	
Biddy, H. (2003). *The death of the environment*. London, England: Oxford University Press.	Book
Bronson, P. (2003, March 4). What is valued most: Our health or our pockets? *The International Herald Tribune*, p. C2.	Article in a newspaper
Dalton, M., & Anderson, J. (2004). Genetically modified food. *The American Scientist, 37*, 12–14.	Article in a scholastic journal
Gleason, A. (2002, January 12). Court to rule on genetic engineering. *The Atlanta Journal-Constitution*, p. B5. Retrieved January 13, 2005, from http://www.accessatlanta.com/ajc	Online document with publication date
Goodwin, A., & Hamilton, T. (n.d.). Crops can be worse for environment. *New Scientist Online News*. Retrieved January 10, 2005, from http://www.newscientist.com/news/news.jsp?id=ns9994283	Online document without a publication date. Use "n.d." for "no date."
Improving taste with growth. (n.d.). Retrieved December 26, 2004, from http://www.onlinescient.org/research/19340/ar5.html	Online document with no author identified and with no publication date
	Personal communications, such as interviews and surveys, are not included in your reference list.

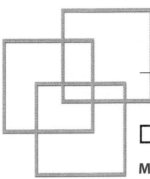

Appendix 4

☐ Logical Organizers

Most academic writing is made up of complex sentences. Academic writers also use other sentence types, such as simple sentences and compound sentences, for special effects. If you need to review the grammar of these sentence types, visit the website for this book at http://esl.college.hmco.com/students.

Compound sentences are used when the writer connects two simple sentences and joins them with either a coordinating conjunction or a transition word. Writers form complex sentences when they combine two simple sentences with a subordinating conjunction.

Use the following chart to guide you when creating compound and complex sentences. Try to use a variety of logical organizers in your writing.

Meaning of Logical Organizers	Compound sentences use:		Complex sentences use:
	Coordinating Conjunctions	**Transition Words**	**Subordinating Conjunctions**
Addition	and	additionally also furthermore in addition moreover	
Cause	for		as because due to the fact that since *Note: as a result of, because of,* and *due to* are followed by a noun phrase, not a clause.
Choice	nor or	instead on the other hand	
Clarification		in essence in other words that is to clarify to illustrate	
Comparison (showing similarities)	and	also by comparison likewise similarly	just as
Concession	yet	however nevertheless nonetheless	although despite the fact that even though in spite of the fact that *Note: despite* and *in spite of* are followed by a noun phrase, not a clause.
Condition			if when unless

Meaning of Logical Organizers	Compound sentences use:		Complex sentences use:
	Coordinating Conjunctions	Transition Words	Subordinating Conjunctions
Contrast (showing differences)	but	by comparison however in comparison in contrast on the other hand	whereas while
Effect or result	so	as a consequence as a result consequently hence therefore thus	if when
Emphasis		as a matter of fact in fact indeed more importantly	
Example		for example for instance to illustrate	
Summary or conclusion		in conclusion in short in summary finally to conclude to sum up overall	
Time		then	after before since when while

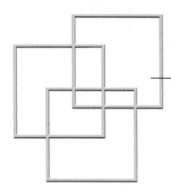

Index

L

largely, 136
Length, of sentences, 172–176
Library resources, 59–60, 105, 192–193
Lists, 100
Logical organizers
    in analytical reports, 52
    in argumentative essays, 228, 231–232
    in expository essays, 22
    in expository reports, 181
    in persuasive essays, 115, 132

M

mainly, 136
majority of, 134
many, 135
"Marking up" pages, 49
may, 135
might, 135
Modal auxiliaries, 135
Modern Language Association (MLA) citation style, 10
most, 134
Multimedia materials, 59

N

Newspapers, 148–150
Non-controversial statements, 37
none, 135
Non-restrictive relative clauses, 35–36
Note taking
    in active reading, 49
    charts for, 204–209
    on controversial issues, 188
    for expository essays, 12, 17
    in sharing information, 64
Noun phrases, 73–75
Nouns, 35, 86
Number forms, 83–84

O

Observations, 7

often, 136
Opinions. *See also* Surveys
    in argumentative essays, 188
    expert, 7. *See also* Credibility, of experts
    in expository reports, 167
    in persuasive essays, 101, 109–110, 128
    strength of, 134–138
Organization charts, 18–21
Outlines, 9, 25

P

Paragraphs. *See* Background paragraphs; Body paragraphs; Concluding paragraphs; Introductory paragraphs; Refuting counterarguments
Parallelism, 170, 176–177
Paraphrasing, 28, 81–90
    attribution signals in, 85
    connecting words in, 85
    credibility of experts by, 35
    definition structures in, 84–85
    number forms in, 83–84
    in persuasive essays, 138
    proper nouns in, 86
    supporting information, 89–90
    synonyms in, 83
    techniques of, 86–89
    word forms in, 82
    word order in, 84
Parentheses [( )], 52, 61, 70
Peer feedback
    of analytical reports, 79–80, 92
    of argumentative essays, 225, 236–237, 242
    of expository essays, 31–32, 44
    of expository reports, 162–163, 179–180, 182
    of persuasive essays, 118, 139

perhaps, 136
Period (.), 9, 227, 231
Persuasive essays, 94–141
    analyzing, 128–133
    body paragraphs for, 138
    drafting, 116–117, 139
    editing, 119
    finalizing, 140
    focusing and organizing information for, 110–116
        background paragraphs for, 113–116
        essay maps and thesis statements for, 111–113
    gathering information for, 97–110
        advanced online searches as, 103–105
        body paragraphs for, 98–100
        discussing as, 97, 102
        interviewing as, 105–108
        lists for, 100
        opinions in, 101, 109–110
        reading as, 97–98
    opinion strength in, 134–138
    peer feedback of, 118, 139
    plagiarism and, 119–121
    practice in, 140–141
    revising, 117, 119, 139
    self-assessment in, 140–141
    summarizing in, 121–128
Plagiarism, 119–121
Points of view, 138
Practice
    on analytical reports, 93
    on argumentative essays, 243
    on expository essays, 45
    on expository reports, 182–183
    on persuasive essays, 140–141
Predictions, 132, 238